Classic Steam

Classic Steam

A superb collection of pictures

Specially selected from the archives of the

YORKSHIRE POST

Edited by Allen Rowley

The Breedon Books
Publishing Company
Derby

First published in Great Britain by
The Breedon Books Publishing Company Limited
44 Friar Gate, Derby, DE1 1DA.
1997

ISBN 1 85983 103 6

Printed and bound by Butler & Tanner, Frome, Somerset.
Jacket printed by Lawrence Allen Ltd, Weston-super-Mare, Somerset.
Colour film by RPS Ltd of Leicester.

Contents

Acknowledgements

In compiling this book the author received considerable assistance from the following staff of Yorkshire Post Newspapers: Mrs Jane Tansey, Photographic Administrator, along with John Hepworth, Gary Lodge and David Siviour of YPN Studios; Miss Jayne Marsden, Deputy Chief Librarian; YPN photographers past and present; Steve Allinson, General Promotions and Publicity Manager YPN, and members of his staff.

He also records his thanks to: Alan Smith, Chairman of Leeds Model Railway Society and long-time professional railway engineer; Peter Rose, whose photographic (railway) memory and photographic skills are renowned; Robert E. Gehrt, former Vice-President Public Relations, Santa Fe Southern Pacific Railway Corporation; Admiral D. Karr, of the Kansas City Southern Railway; and to a long-time friend, Yorkshire-born Derek Scrafton, who has contributed so much to railways and travel worldwide, but particularly in Canada and Australia. He lives in Adelaide where he retired in April 1997, as Director-General of Transport for South Australia (but still has an avid interest in British railways, particularly in the North of England).

The author pays particular tribute to the late Mr Wilfred Taylor, former Photographic Manager of Yorkshire Post Newspapers, for his foresight in ensuring that the glass negatives from which most of the pictures in this book were made, were placed in safe hands.

Lastly, but certainly not least, the author records his particular thanks to his wife, Joyce, for her help with research - and for her patience.

Photographic Purchases

Copies of photographs appearing in this book which are the copyright of Yorkshire Post Newspapers may be obtained from the Yorkshire Post Photo Sales Department (telephone: 0113-243-2701, Ext 1360). Negative numbers for such pictures appear at the end of the captions. Where negatives are no longer available, this is shown as: (Neg.N/A). Wherever possible, sources of other photographs are also shown with the captions. The publishers are grateful for permission to use all these pictures.

Foreword

by Andrew Scott

Head of the National Railway Museum

THE STEAM railway meant a lot to Yorkshire. The world's very first steam railway brought coal from Middleton Colliery down into Leeds in 1812. Since then the county's industries of engineering, mining, textiles and agriculture have all depended on the dense network of railways which spread across the region in the 19th century. Old and new communities alike thrived on the new accessibility and soon the railways were the arteries carrying the very life blood of the county.

By the 1950s, the railway was in decline as the added flexibility of motor transport became attractive. On reflection, it had changed very little in the previous century. But change came fast in the 1960s, transforming the railway to a network of core passenger and freight services, operating — compared to the standards of the steam age — with a ruthless efficiency.

Although it is fashionable to criticise today's railways, for the most part they offer a more efficient and reliable service than ever before. From the standpoint of the York traveller like myself, trains every half hour to and from London — and Newcastle — and every hour to and from Manchester Airport represent a conveyor belt service unimagined even as recently as the 1960s.

What the railways have gained in efficiency as people carriers - which is, after all, what they are there for — they have lost in diversity. Today, less than 40 trains of only two different types carry far more traffic between King's Cross, Leeds, York and Edinburgh than the hundreds of steam locomotives of more than a dozen different designs which they replaced. The diversity of the steam age railway was at once fascinating and desperately inefficient. Add in the shunters which used to bring empty trains in and out of the terminals, the even greater diversity of local trains and the whole lost world of local freight operations — and the unending fascination of the steam age railway begins to make sense.

Classic Steam reminds us of this lost world. The *Yorkshire Post's* photographers — and several guest photographers — have recorded what at the time was the mundane daily scene. Today, their quality images, most of them painstakingly shot on glass plates, provide us with a glimpse of a world which some of us will remember, and which others will see for the first time.

We can take it as read that railway enthusiasts will enjoy the new insights to be found within these pages but I hope a wider audience will enjoy it too. Look beyond the number on the locomotive's cabside and see something of that lost world: a world in which many thousands of dedicated men and women worked in difficult conditions to keep the freight and passenger trains moving and to keep Yorkshire at work; a world which affected the landscape of every town, village and workplace. Today, from the Sprinter speeding through the West Riding to Manchester Airport, we get only hints of that world, buried beneath the greenery — or the industrial estates — which have grown up over the old goods yards. Read these pages and you will discover a real flavour of a world now totally changed.

Introduction

by Allen Rowley

A SHORT time ago, a group of international railway enthusiasts which holds regular meetings in North Yorkshire, was discussing 'the good old days' and making the inevitable comparisons between railway systems, and the changes which have occurred between then and the present day.

A fairly widely-travelled bunch, with a corresponding range of railway interests, they are, nevertheless, ever aware that it was the inventive skills of British engineers which put the nation in the forefront of a new form of transport which was to revolutionise the way people and goods were moved in countries all around the globe.

It was to be over a century before the jet engine brought about a similar revolution.

Some people would disagree with the oft-heard claim that the British created what was for years probably the best railway system in the world. And it would also seem to be the case that, as with so many other fine British inventions, those same engineers often received more recognition, and more opportunity to progress their developments, by going abroad, than they did in the 'old country'.

However, their claim that British was best can still be substantiated by the fact that, in countries around the

Whilst the Stockton & Darlington and Liverpool and Manchester railways were still over the horizon, Leeds had a form of railway. An Act of Parliament of 1758 authorised the building of a waggonway between the Manor of Middleton, south of the town 'to supply the inhabitants of Leeds with coals for their use and consumption'. Charles Brandling, of Gosforth Hall, near Killingworth, had experience of wooden waggonways on Tyneside and his inheritance of estates and collieries at Middleton put him on the road to fame and fortune. His double-track line from Middleton to Casson Close, near Leeds Bridge, is shown in part in this engraving, with Christ Church behind the coal staiths. This pioneer line, to a gauge of 4ft 1in, was converted to standard gauge in 1881. It established another record when it became the first standard gauge line to be successfully preserved by amateurs, the Middleton Preservation Society running its first train on June 20, 1960, Much development has been carried-out on the line which is a popular attraction with enthusiasts and members of the public alike. *Neg.No.0Y159.*

Yorkshire-built is well built. Messrs Todd, Kitson & Laird built this locomotive, named 'Lion', in Leeds in 1837. Just over 100 years later, in 1938, it was pictured in action at London's Euston Station celebrating the centenary of the London & Birmingham Railway. The engine later appeared in the film *The Titfield Thunderbolt*, in a starring role. *Neg.No.RAIL 24.*

An interesting slice of Victorian life at Crossgates Station in the Leeds eastern suburbs: a somewhat battered chaise longue, a pole and a wooden ladder (perhaps evidence of early debris-dropping by vandals on this line) are at the rear of the platform. In the background a jolly group of young ladies is being given the once-over by a young blade in a straw boater who cuts a fine stance leaning on his brolly. As for the 'bit of a toff' standing by the engine: Mike Scargill, membership secretary of the Middleton Railway, and a footplate crew member, who saw this picture in the Spring 1997 edition of *Portraits of Steam*, suggested the fellow was probably a commercial traveller. As such, he would have held a full Commercial Traveller's Ticket, which would entitle him to full porters' assistance to expedite changing trains with all his luggage (of which there is a fair pile in the background). *Neg. N/A*

world, there are numerous examples of decades-old British railway products in use today; and countless rusting relics that well-served their time bearing 'British Made' plates.

Among the group of enthusiasts mentioned above was a chap who recalled those who used to argue that railway development in the UK — certainly in terms of passenger equipment — might well have compared more favourably with the best overseas, had it not been for World War Two. But some years before that conflict, argued someone else, there were passenger cars (coaches) in the USA which, in terms of passenger comfort and amenities, were far ahead of the then latest equipment being produced in the UK.

On the other hand, another member of the group proudly recalled that as a boy, in the 1930s, when Gresley's world-famous A4 streamlined 'Pacifics' were being teamed-up with sets of smart, matching coaches on what is now the East Coast Main Line, the latest piece of Japanese technology he had come across was a garish, tin 'put-put' boat (the sound it made) powered by a small container which burned methylated spirits, as it lurched around his mother's washing-up bowl!

Unfortunately for him, his patriotic contribution was immediately knocked back when another chap produced a railway magazine picturing 1997-style Japanese main-line railway equipment which makes even their famous 'Bullet Trains' look dated. As for the disgraceful 'slam door' rolling stock still in daily use in Britain; it looks positively prehistoric by comparison.

And yet if that same slam-door stock, or something similar, is attached to a preserved steam locomotive belching smoke and bits of grit, then given the option, many youngsters — who today can handle electronic equipment which oft-baffles their parents, let alone their grandparents — would likely choose to ride in one of its old compartments, sporting fading pictures of seaside towns of half-a-century ago, and equipped with seats little more comfortable than the horsehair-stuffed versions they replaced; rather than choose a Japanese job looking like an advanced Airbus fuselage on wheels, Such is the lure of steam!

Until the last decade or so, no other form of transport had acquired quite the same all-round appeal among all classes and genders as had the railway train.

Perhaps it goes back some 150 years to its liberating

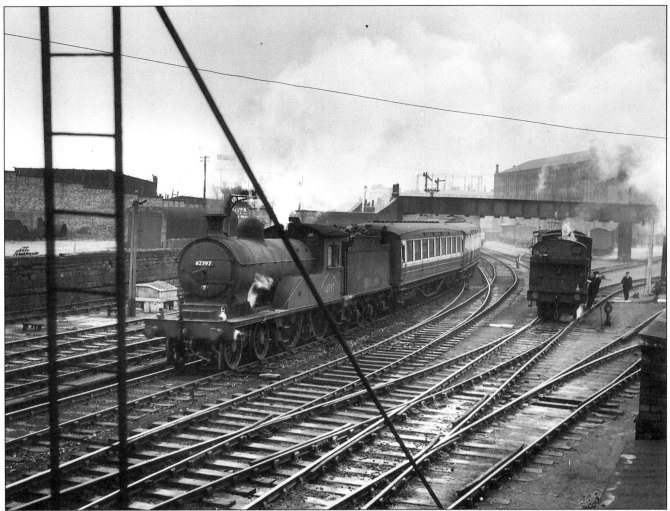

Introduced into service in 1899, over half-a-century before this picture was taken, Class D20 4-4-0 No.62397 is heading a York-bound train round the Marsh Lane Curve, Leeds. This was the site of the Leeds terminus of the Leeds & Selby Railway, opened in September 1834. *Neg.No.8/C603.*

Queen Victoria was still on the throne when the North Eastern Railway turned out 110 of these locomotives from Darlington Works. British Railways' No.67262 lasted long enough to run in the reign of the present Queen and is pictured at Leeds City in 1953. *Neg.N/A*

effect on rural folk, in particular, whose travel had previously been limited to a once-a-week horse and cart, or pony and trap ride into the next village or town — if they were lucky — until the 'iron road' provided a network of opportunities in Britain to travel between thousands of country town and city stations.

For countless thousands, then millions, the 'seaside' became not a picture on a postcard but the real thing, a thing of wonder to which one could go, have a good time, and be back home again the same day. And in the big cities, ever-spreading, ordinary folk could more regularly be reunited with relatives who had moved house 'all the way' from, say, Salford to Wilmslow, or Leeds to Huddersfield, and so on.

At the same time, the comparison that we can now fly from Leeds to Gatwick in less time than it took by those early trains to travel from Leeds to Selby is meaningless; for despite their slow speeds, the leap from stage coach and canal barge travel to such trains was a much bigger feat for those early passengers. Today, we *expect* development, although as with the Japanese example cited above, some get it faster than others!

Naturally, not only was 'people travel' improved. The carriage of goods, particularly in bulk, expanded rapidly and farms, mines, engineering and chemical plants and thousands of other businesses were linked into the system. Both goods and passenger trains speeded-up the carriage of milk, mail, livestock, parcels and people going to and from work (although the words 'parcel' and 'people' have unfortunate connotations at the time of writing)

Some would say that this also applies to air travel, especially where the slick but packed fuselages of aircraft on charter flights — and the hassle in and around many airports begin to slow down transport progress and become a feature of daily life.

These are hardly situations to create the folklore, legends, pride, sense of duty, loyalty and yes, even the romance, which grew up with the trains and blossomed at the height of the steam era. Travel then was still an adventure for the many — and particularly the younger set - and it lasted up to around the 1960s, perhaps because it was not too closely geared to the profit-influenced purgatory of Economy Class in particular, which has tended to permeate air travel this last two decades.

And the trains were always closer to the people. In the cities they were everywhere and even if you travelled only country roads, you were bound to be involved with, or influenced by, their infrastructure every few miles. Round the clock, 365 days a year, whether in town or country, you could not go for long without seeing, hearing — even smelling — steam train activity. Of course, that 'aroma'

was manna to the enthusiast, and in particular small boys.

The railways brought a whole new lifestyle for countless families. Most schoolchildren from before the turn of the century until the 1960s knew somebody who had a father/brother/uncle/cousin who worked on the railway, even if they did not have one in their own family. And such workers were often pillars of society, much-respected, responsible and considerate, especially the drivers who, many would say, were in their time on a higher pinnacle of fame with schoolboys than even today's airline pilots.

If the railways were close to the British, they were even more appealing to residents of countries like Canada and the USA, where they were a lifeline for the folks in the 'boondocks' and the deserts; in the mountains and out on the muskeg, whose towns could be several hundred miles from the next place of any size.

My long-time and much-missed friend, the late Dr Bob Sprenger, used to recall that there were two big daily happenings in the small town where he was raised on the seemingly unending Manitoba prairie: one was the arrival and departure of the Canadian Pacific's morning westbound 'Mail and Express' train (carrying mail and parcels); the other was the arrival and departure of the evening eastbound, hopefully rewarding similar expectations.

"As kids, we used to go down to the depot and see them every day," he used to recall. "We knew every engineer, fireman, conductor and brakeman. We could hardly believe that, at the end of the line, nearly two thousand miles way, there was the ocean — something we prairie-bound youngsters could barely imagine because we had never seen any stretch of water bigger than a prairie farmer's pond."

The same situation applied across much of the USA, and of such stuff were made the songs that covered a whole spectrum of railroad activity, from construction: *I've Been Working on the Railroad*; through operation: *The Wabash Cannonball*; pleasant times: *The Hobo's Lullaby*; to destruction: *Wreck of the Old '97*.

And the great trains became part of the British culture, their names known to also almost every citizen: 'The Flying Scotsman', the 'Golden Arrow', 'Silver Jubilee' and 'Coronation' among them.

And back across the Atlantic, the proud passenger trains made up of Pullman cars, or superb stainless-steel cars with fluted sides, carried proud names: 'The Empire Builder', 'City of San Francisco', 'Spirit of St Louis', '20th Century Limited', 'Orange Blossom Special' and the 'Gulf Coast Rebel', to name but a few.

Wherever these trains went, the legends grew, for until

Taken well over 30 years ago, this photograph is of 'Windle', a shunter donated to the Middleton Railway, Leeds, by Pilkington Brothers Ltd, glass manufacturers, in 1961. *Neg.No.RAIL 21*

the arrival of the electric telegraph, the trains literally carried the news as arriving passengers updated western pioneers on what was going on 'back east'. The same had happened in England, for the trains were faster than the stage coaches and arrived more frequently.

As the railways grew in size and importance, so did the objects (in the kindest sense of the word) of people's attention at every station: the engines. For youngsters in particular, these were the objects of desire 'the things that made it all go'.

And as the engines grew in size and importance, their footplate crews took an heroic stance in the eyes of their young fans. One can almost imagine that had today's football club marketing specialists been around 60 or more years ago, and applied their talents to specialised clothing for engine drivers and firemen, every lad in the land would have wanted a replica. As it is, railroad T-shirts covered in the logos, colour schemes and pictures of engines of famous US railroads, even long-gone 'fallen flag' lines, are a feature of daily life in America today.

The railway nostalgia and memorabilia businesses are

very big indeed in most developed countries; so is the associated publishing of books and magazines and the production of souvenirs for sale at preserved railway centres and other outlets.

Although the ranks of train spotters are not so numerous as in the steam days — and the unthinking, mind–blanking attitude of the 'chattering classes' on TV and radio might, sadly, have played some part in this — overall, and in every strata of society from bishops to bus drivers, world-famous names (eg Frank Sinatra) to housewives (one of the finest, and most unusual model railways in the UK exhibition circuit was part-built and is operated by a woman), railways — and in particular those of the steam era — have a lasting appeal.

In an age when driving anywhere by car is becoming more of a toil than a pleasure for many people, those old enough to recall the enormous pleasure of seeing the British countryside at its best (if only because from a train it was possible to see more of it than is ever possible from a car) can only hope that such joys might well be restored if the privatised railway companies can put the same dedication and effort into their businesses as did their steam age predecessors when it was often much harder than now to return a profit.

What, I hope, becomes clear to the reader of this publication is that the compiler set out, through the use of many of the Yorkshire Post Newspapers' *Yorkshire Steam Collection* of pictures — which have held such a long-term appeal for those who have viewed them in 'bits and pieces' — to produce a book which will have a much wider appeal than a straightforward technical treatise or engineering insight; a publication which will appeal to young and old alike and provide fuel for learning for the former and pleasurable nostalgia for the latter.

The particular interests of railway-influenced people today are wide and varied. Some collect 'railwayana' (including buttons, signal lamps, engine name plates, promotional posters of yesteryear, and so on). Others specialise in old photographs, or copies thereof; books, videotapes, cassettes of steam and diesel sounds, transparencies, handbills and even PR releases.

Apart from locomotives, rolling stock and infrastructure, my own railway interests lie in the part they have played in the history and development of nations large and small; their effect upon the landscape, and in the viewing of great trains passing through some of the world's finest and most dramatic scenery, be it in Britain, the USA, Canada or Australia.

So this book is really an historic ramble around railways and their surroundings, showing what could be seen in the days when we had time to stop and stare, and admire, and be proud of the men and machines that combined to make the great days of *Classic Steam* worthy of recall.

If it does that, we will have fully answered countless requests from enthusiasts in many countries who have long urged us to produce an omnibus edition of pictures from the YPN Yorkshire Steam Collection and the Yorkshire Post's *Portraits of Steam* special editions.

All the 'Steam Tales' in this publication have appeared in various editions of *Portraits of Steam* and are one of its more popular features.

How The Railways Changed Lives

C. Lockhart.

THERE can be no doubt that the steam railway locomotive played a very important part in bringing prosperity to many parts of England. It enabled large works to be set up where previously there were few jobs other than in agriculture. What few other jobs there were meant that many people spent all their lives in the area where they were born.

The railways changed all that and folk moved around more for work and pleasure. Reasonably cheap travel meant they could more easily reach more pleasant parts of the country.

In particular, I have in mind the old Great Central Railway which plied between Leicester and Cleethorpes. Originally this was the Lancashire, Derbyshire & East Coast Railway. It served an area where the Duke of Newcastle, the Duke of Portland and other landed gentry had very extensive estates, large areas of which were open to the public.

I served my apprenticeship as a locomotive fitter and turner at a little railway workshop at Tuxford, north Nottinghamshire. This quiet little area had a complex of railway stations. One of them was called The Dukeries, and at this point the Great Central crossed over the Great Northern Railway (later the LNER).

King Edward VII was said to have visited the Dukeries area as a guest of one of the landed gentry and, for many years after I started work there, we had an engine which bore the royal coat-of-arms and was said to be always available when King Edward travelled from London on the Great Northern.

He would change trains at Dukeries Junction and complete his journey to The Dukeries on the Great Central.

The line is now closed, but for years it carried many excursion trains to Cleethorpes and there was often a stream of trains carrying export coal to Immingham.

Mr Lockhart, now 96, lives at Braithwell, Rotherham.

An Image To Fit The Curve

BACK in the 1940s, when steam was probably making its greatest contribution ever to the British nation, if 'great curves' were mentioned to servicemen, they were unlikely to remind them of a particular section of railway track.

More likely to spring to mind were Betty Grable, Rita Hayworth or Lana Turner — or even Mae West if large radius curves were more to their fancy.

Publicity pictures of these stars — and dozens more like them — adorned corners of barrack blocks, works canteens, Nissen and Quonset huts and the depths of great ships at sea. Most originated as publicity stills issued by film companies. And it was in the realms of publicity that such pictures and those of the railways came close together,

The advantage of a picture of a train on a curve is that it is less formal or 'starchy', and from a publicity point of view it gives a much better impression of the vehicles down the length of the train.

So when the masters of the art — the Atchison, Tope-ka & Santa Fe, Union Pacific and Pennsylvania Railroads in the USA; and the Canadian Pacific in Canada — set out to promote their streamliners, dome cars, sleepers and what-have-you, they found that locations with curves provided the best results; especially when a speeding train took on a leaning appearance.

So much so that those very same curves are now the favourite locations for picturing freight trains; even better if a reverse curve can be worked in to contain the snake-like appearance of a train that can be over a mile long: witness CP Railway's shots of coal trains at Cathedral Rock on the Great Divide.

The *Yorkshire Post* photographers who took most of the pictures in our *Yorkshire Steam Collection* had their favourite locations and if you can imagine any one of these trains coming at the camera in a straight line rather than around a curve, you can see the advantage of a curvaceous approach; as the film director might have said of the starlet…

A2/2 Class No.60503 'Lord President' catches the glint of frosty winter sunshine on the way north out of York with a Leeds-Newcastle train on December 29, 1952. Sharp and shivery outside those coaches; muggy but comfortable inside — and thoughts of Hogmanay uppermost in many a passenger's mind, even if they were only near-cousins of the Scots. *Neg.No.12/C677.*

Same place, same day, different train. The lingering sun catches a rake of surprisingly clean coaches on the great curve which still launches trains northward from York's superb (and curved) train shed. What a pity more 'spit and polish' had not been applied to the grimy, 'a11 angles and bits 'n pieces' locomotive: 43097, a 2-6-0 Ivatt Class 4. *Neg.No.11/C677*

Curves a-plenty for this up-market equipment: headed by A3 'Pacific' 60074 'Harvester', eight Pullman cars trail the engine which bears the plate: 'The Queen of Scots' ahead of its chimney. It was just one of the Pullman trains which served Harrogate and Leeds for many years. Its route from Glasgow to London was not the fastest way of getting from A to B, but it was certainly one of the more pleasant ones, especially on such a nice day. *Neg.No.BIW/86*

She'll be coming round the mountain when she comes …well, not quite a mountain, just the embankment alongside the tracks skirting Copley Hill Depot, Leeds, allowing a sweeping view of V2 No.60865 with a train of mixed stock. The V2s were equally at home on passenger or goods trains. *Neg.No.18/C652*

Leaning into the curve in a style reminiscent of publicity pictures of the magnificent 'Pacifics' of the French NORD system; or a 'super-elevated transition camera angle' as American railroad fans might say, ex-LNER A3 No.60080 'Dick Turpin' has an exhaust as clean as the proverbial whistle as it comes around the track's curvature at Helwith Bridge in August, 1959, with 'The Thames-Clyde Express'. In the late 1950s and 60s, as diesels steadily displaced steam, some of the remaining steam locomotives found themselves switched to 'foreign parts' before eventual withdrawal. For a time, trains from Leeds to Carlisle and Glasgow, which had previously had former LMS engines at the front end, found ex-LNER equipment such as this in charge. *Neg.No.B1W2*

'Royal Scot' No.46137 'The Prince of Wales's Volunteers (South Lancashire)' was either a very hard-working engine determined to make its presence felt in White Rose country, or it was a favourite with the photographers, for it appears many times in the Yorkshire Post Newspapers' *Yorkshire Steam Collection.* Here it is again, passing Farnley with a Liverpool-Newcastle train, a thin covering of snow reflecting the gloom of a winter's day. To many, the small chimney looked out of proportion with the bulk of the front end of the then un-rebuilt class. This locomotive was later rebuilt and, in common with the rest of the class, equipped with taper boiler and curved smoke deflectors ('wind cutters') to many fans. *Neg.No.2/7445*

Just to prove this publication is not entirely biased toward Yorkshire, and that there were some lovely curves in the land of the Red Rose (and not all of them in Blackpool Tower ballroom), here's a train from Manchester approaching Southport behind 'Black Five' No.44728. Mind you, the trackwork on the right looks a wee bit 'iffy' to anyone who knew York in its heyday. Compare it with the picture above (right). *Neg.No.BIW 8*

And here's York's great northern curve from another angle. Some great British strengths are to be seen in this picture of A4 'Pacific' No.60023 'Golden Eagle', chime whistle sounding its haunting wail as it eases a train of at least 12 coaches into the station in December, 1952. The spacious track layout, colour light signals, powerful locomotive and length and weight of train on this Newcastle-King's Cross express add importance to the occasion. As for the 'VIROL' advertisement on the extreme right, well that too was a British tradition. After a brief stop, the Blaydon racer will pound south through Notts, Lincs, Cambs and Herts and be safely tucked away in its London shed before Big Ben chimes for the Nine O'Clock News. *Neg.No.5/C677*

First you would hear a sort of 'twanging' noise on the rails, then a drumming sound and a noise like someone suffering a series of fast sneezes; then a 2-6-4 tank, No.42052, came bowling bunker first through Kirkstall on the way from Bradford to Leeds on a four-track line that made you realise it was nearing somewhere important, like Leeds City Station. June 24, 1952. *Neg.No.4/C642*

Passengers who had enjoyed a successful day's racing would be looking forward to getting back to the pubs of Otley and Ilkley (those who had lost might have been hopeful of being invited along), as this returning Wetherby Races special eased off the main line at Arthington North and on to the Otley curve, with immaculate B16 No.61478 in charge in the summer of 1958. *Neg.No.B1W35*

STEAM TALES

Run Rabbit, Run Rabbit, Run, Run, Run…

William C.Addy

APART from the marvellous scenery on the Settle-Carlisle line, it was very hard work firing heavy goods trains, but I enjoyed the trips. Always a bonus were the fresh eggs, mushrooms (pick your own) and the fresh caught wild rabbits, we were able to obtain.

In those days, some locos were very cantankerous and taxed the skill of the fireman; others would steam easily – "Just show her the shovel …"

But if steam pressure started to fall, it meant stopping until it could be built-up again, which could take about 15 to 20 minutes. You always stopped at a signal box, for communication. In the case of a following passenger train, it meant backing into the sidings. This gave crews of following trains a bit of time to go into the signal box for some eggs and a couple of rabbits.

The cost of the rabbits was five shillings. They were caught by the signalmen in traps around the signal-box area. There were some days when no trains were able to stop, so the signalman would hang the rabbits over the handrail which ran around the box windows. Now, the timekeeping of trains – even goods trains – in those days was very strict, to the minute, and the signalmen reported every train as it passed to Control.

At times like these, if my mate and I wanted a rabbit, the driver slowed down (remember it was a heavy train), and I got down on to the bottom step, jumped off, ran across the adjoining rail, sprinted up the signal-box steps banged five bob on the table, grabbed a pair of rabbits, shot down the steps, sprinted about 50 yards after my engine, dived across the main line jumped on the step and threw the rabbits on to the footplate. Then I had to stoke up again to catch up on the slightly flagging steam.

Phew!!!

Mr Addy started work at Stourton Loco sheds in 1934 and was one of six members of the same family based there during World War Two. His father was a driver, a sister worked as a labourer. William eventually became a driver on Leeds to Manchester, Liverpool and Blackpool trains. He was awarded the BEM in 1974 and retired in 1980 as a TopLink driver on HSTs between Leeds, Bradford, Harrogate and Kings Cross. He lives at Parkstone Grove, Leeds.

The Glory Machines

SUPERPOWER is not a description which might have been uttered by the likes of Sir Nigel Gresley, Archibald Sturrock, R.E.L. Maunsell or Sir William Stanier, despite their association with the design of large engines, but had it been in vogue in their day, no doubt someone would have chosen it to describe the engines pictured in this section.

At Leeds Central on March 18, 1948, 'Andrew K. McCosh' had a purposeful look about it, eager to be up and running. The imposing A4 was originally numbered 4494 and named 'Osprey', but it was later renamed to commemorate a railway director. When the picture was taken it still sported LNER on its tender. The 'No.3' on its front end came from a 1946 re-numbering scheme but British Railways eventually settled for 60003. *Neg.No.1/258C*

'Going like the wind', was an oft-used expression to describe a train travelling at speed. One might say then that 'Hal O' The Wynd' was well-named, for the plume from its safety valve shows that A1 60116 had plenty of power available to speed 'The Queen of Scots Pullman' on its journey. 'Hal' is pictured on the way to Leeds Central to pick up the Pullman on October 8, 1951. *Neg.No.5/C594*

Designer Sir Vincent Raven had every right to be proud of his products and skills when his name was cast in tablets of metal and 'Pacific' 60126 was named after him. The Newcastle-based engine was caught on camera at Neville Hill, Leeds, on November 27, 1951. *Neg.No.10/C607*

The stovepipe chimney of A2 60539 'Bronzino' marks the spot where most of the by-products of the coal she had just taken aboard at Neville Hill, Leeds, would finally exit this splendid machine. November 27, 1951. *Neg.No.2/C607*

Now you see it, now you don't — a glorious piece of gleaming machinery: but appearances are not always what they seem. Nameplates and cab numbers indicate that this is LMS 6100 'The Royal Scot' (first of its class), all set to sail to the USA for the Chicago World's Fair in 1933. Actually, it was another engine in disguise whose name and number were swapped with the real 'The Royal Scot' for the American tour. Whatever the reason, the directors of the LMS no doubt assumed that the large numbers of Americans claiming even the remotest links with the British Royal Family and the countless thousands who had genuine Scottish pedigrees would be pleased with this product of the UK. Introduced in 1927, engines of the class were superheated, with Parallel boiler. The engine of the version pictured weighed 84 tons 18cwt. Pressure: 250lbs; Cylinders: three 18ins x 26ins; Driving wheels: 6ft x 9ins. *Neg.No.RAIL 19*

An American prominent in the aircraft manufacturing business once said of his British counterparts: 'How come they can produce beautiful-looking aircraft, then clutter the cockpit with after-thought brackets, bits of piping and plating?' Examine this picture closely and you will note the habit was not confined to the aviation industry: Here is A1 60120 'Kittiwake' positively gleaming in the sun at Wortley, Leeds, on October 17, 1951. Let your eye travel back along the superbly turned-out motion to the nicely-angled flush-fitting of the cab and streamlined casing and there we go — what looks like a piece of old rope snakes along the running plate before disappearing into the 'innards'. Before any former cleaners burst with pride at the turnout of the engine, it should be pointed out that she had just been given a fresh coat of paint in the then new British Railways' express passenger engine livery. *Neg.No.14/C596*

A much later product, but not quite so resplendent: one suspects the designers of British Railways' new standard type 'Pacifics' of the 'Britannia' Class had taken more than a passing glance at then current North American, German and French locomotive development when putting their thoughts together. Traces of them all can be seen, from the near-Teutonic front-end to the near-all-weather cab and North American outside plumbing of a slightly grimy 70032 'Tennyson' on January 1, 1953. Nevertheless, it was setting a style for Britain. But sadly it was all too late as the throbbing diesels hove in sight. *Neg.No.3/C678*

The final two pictures in this section are separated by some 30 years but were taken within a few yards of each other at Leeds City Station. Here, an immaculate 46117 of the 'Royal Scot' Class, named 'Welsh Guardsman', is let down by its tender having, apparently, been filled following the cleaning operation. Still, it's great stuff, no doubt much-appreciated by the 'spotters' at the end of the platform on a cool day in 1958. *Neg.No.BIW 13*

Three decades on and the preserved 'Princess Coronation' Class 7P 46229 'Duchess of Hamilton' looks ready for a racing start under the wires. With a special train in tow, this loco was fast enough to scorn the electrics which had super-seded steam and the diesels, Introduced in 1937, these engines weighed 105 tons 5cwt (plus another three tons when streamlined) and were ar-guably the most powerful passenger locos in Britain. Pressure: 250lbs; Cylinders: (four) 16ins x 28ins; Driving wheels: 6ft 9ins; Tractive effort: 40,000lbs. *Neg.No.134902/6A*

Runaway Trolley

J.Waters

ON leaving school, my first job was that of junior porter at Kirkstall Station, Leeds. I was there for 12 months and met some very interesting, likeable and helpful people. One of the senior porters was called Rodger, a fallen gentleman if ever I saw one. He did not stay long enough to get his uniform – not that it bothered him.

He was usually dressed in a camel-hair coat, wore baggy trousers and always wore brown kid gloves, a silk scarf and a trilby! I could tell that he was used to 'better things' by the way that he handled parcels. He would carefully pick them up by the string, using forefinger and thumb, as though they were filled with something rather nasty.

The station booking hall was at road level and the route across to the four long platforms was by way of a long, steep slope, or an enclosed footbridge. All heavy goods were conveyed on large trolleys down the slope, then across the 'sleepered' level crossing at the end of the platforms.

Manoeuvring a fully-laden trolley down the pathway was anything but easy. To check its rate of descent, and prevent it running out of control, it had to be 'scraped' against a specially provided long wooden barrier. This normally worked quite well. Indeed it had to, for a sharp 180 degree turn was required at the foot of the slope.

On one occasion, whilst attempting this difficult manoeuvre, Rodger failed to control the speed of the trolley. I did my best by clinging on to the back – but to no avail. Rodger, walking backwards, was a worried man and increased his strides to combat the weight of the laden trolley. But as we shot towards the bottom of the slope he had obviously decided what to do: he leapt clear as a quarter of a ton trolley, piled high with 56lb boxes of rhubarb, flew off the edge of the platform and crashed down, completely blocking both main lines.

Near panic gripped us for the Bradford to Bristol express was due and always trav-elled at a fair lick through Kirkstall.

Swift action by all hands on the station saw us trying to man-handle the trolley back on to the platform.

This entailed lifting it to shoulder height – or above your head, depending on how tall you were. As I stumbled about in the loose stone ballast, it seemed it was permanently above my head.

The thought that I might end up splat-tered all over the front of the fast-ap-proaching express also helped to turn my legs to near jelly.

Then – a final heave and it was back on the platform and we just had time to move the scattered rhubarb boxes clear of the running line before the express appeared round the bend and we scrambled up on to the platform.

As ever, it was punctual and travelling at speed. What the driver made of the de-bris-strewn track, I never knew. But he should have thanked his lucky stars. I cer-tainly thanked mine!

Mr Waters lives at Swinnow Road,
Leeds

Special Occasions

GOING back to the days of the 'Big Four' (LNER, LMS, Southern Railway and the Great Western Railway) and even earlier, there is plenty of evidence to show that the owners were never slow to grab a publicity opportunity or create a sense of occasion whenever the chance arose.

New structures, new developments, new trains — and particularly locomotive naming ceremonies were always good for a celebration.

In the years between the two world wars, the names chosen were most fitting: famous regiments, football clubs, cities, locomotive designers and members of the British Commonwealth were among those so honoured. Others indicated speed, strength and reliability.

In more recent years, like so many other facets of British life (arguably, the American-style names now applied to Rugby League clubs are a typical example), the naming of diesel locomotives reached almost farcical proportions, BR having fallen into the commercial swamp of charging companies for the 'honour' of having their names on engines. Diesels whose names bore no connection whatsoever with the rural areas or industrial belts through which they roamed, seemed oddly out of place.

Others bore the most appalling, almost gross titles; others were quite ridiculous.

But thank goodness the old railway companies were among those who had the presence of mind to record for posterity such special occasions as those pictured here.

As nameplates go, this V2 had one of the longest. Brigadier-General J.L.J. Clarke, Colonel of the East Yorkshire Regiment, draws back the veil to reveal its name as 'The Snapper, The East Yorkshire Regiment, The Duke of York's Own', at a ceremony in Hull in 1937, prior to the locomotive hauling the Royal Train from Hull to York. *Neg.No.Rail 18*

Another military occasion: even the footplate crew (alongside the tender), appeared to be wearing their medals as Class V2 4843 became 'King's Own Yorkshire Light Infantry' at a Doncaster Plant Works naming ceremony in May, 1939. The First Battalion of the regiment formed the Guard of Honour. A few months later they were off to war. And in due course the chap who compiled this book joined the Fourth Battalion KOYLI (Army Cadet Force) before graduating to the real army: a course of action he could recommend to those of today's youngsters who complain there is nothing for them to do. *Neg.No.Rail 22*

Something to do or not, boys will be boys and perhaps bored with the speeches and the massed ranks of VIPs and others, two young Tykes in short trousers have sneaked along to the end of the podium to peer under the front end of Class V2 4806. The occasion was the naming ceremony, at Richmond Station, North Riding of Yorkshire, of 'The Green Howard, Alexandra, Princess of Wales's Own Yorkshire Regiment' by Major-General H.E. Franklyn. The station's architecturally pleasing overall roof was ablaze with bunting for the occasion in September, 1938. Sadly, not even the Green Howards were able to save this charming country town's station when Dr Beeching's notorious plan closed it — the first step toward today's oft-jammed roads in the Dales and towns like Richmond. *Neg.No.RAIL 28*

This special occasion, at York Station, almost reached Hollywood proportions with bunting and flags everywhere and floodlights set up to highlight the shine on V2 'St Peter's School, A.D.627'. Only a select few of these mixed traffic engines were given names. *Neg.No.678D*

Here is A4 No.4495 'Golden Fleece' which had a short life as 'Great Snipe', ready to depart Leeds Central on September 23, 1937 on a demonstration run of the 'West Riding Limited'. *Neg.No.D376*

An engine with some real class: Great Northern Railway No.1 at London King's Cross in 1938, just before its departure for Stevenage with a special train representing the style of express running at the turn of the century. *Neg.No.1/C681*

At Stevenage the VIPs gathered and were seemingly more interested in the old 4-2-2 than the sleek streamlined casing of 'Sir Nigel Gresley'. The Press made quite a day of the occasion (which marked the 50th anniversary of 'The Flying Scotsman' train) and in today's atmosphere of photographers in baseball caps worn back-to-front, multi-hued bomber jackets and trainers, it seems quite astonishing to see them respectably attired in suits and hats. Those in the battered raincoats were probably reporters. *Neg.No.4/C681*

There would be, of course, always be one photographer calling, "Can I have just one more, Sir?" as both drivers and firemen itched to be under way. *Neg.No.3/C681*

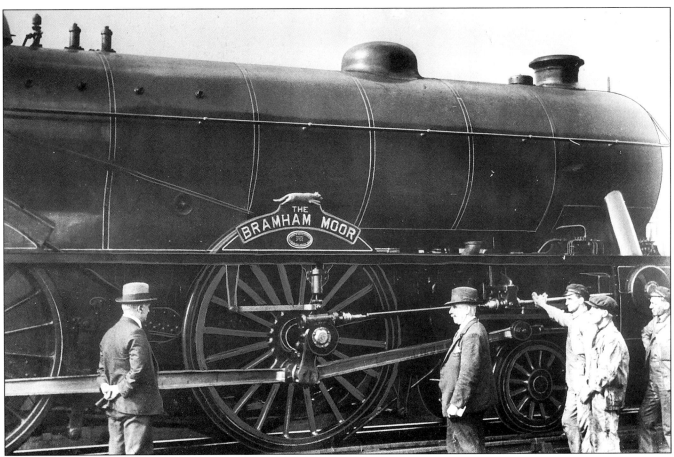

Ready for the road! One of the crew, cleaning rag in hand, leans on the loco as one of the 'gaffers' studies the Lentz rotary valve gear of the pristine 'The Bramham Moor' D49/2 'Hunt' Class engine of the LNER at Leeds in 1932. *Neg.No.RAIL 30*

Settle Station was en fête in November, 1938, for the naming of LMS 'Patriot Class' No.5538 'Giggleswick'. *Neg.No.RAIL 11*

If you think the child on the left looks as if some-one had just told him to 'Hush!' you are half-way to knowing this unusual locomotive's full name. At least, 'Hush-Hush' was the name given by rail-waymen to the LNER's No.10000, a unique ma-rine-boilered creation which emerged from Dar-lington Works in 1929. With a front end that looked like a straight steal from some of France's leading locomotives, its boiler casing would also have done credit to some of the American stream-lined efforts of that era. *Neg.N/A*

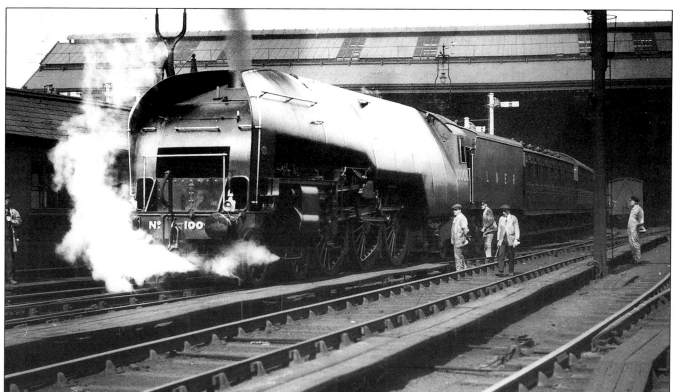

This second view of the 'Hush-Hush' reveals more clearly the engine's 4-6-4 wheel arrangement and also the additional shielding over the smoke box door. The proliferation of hand rails and grab handles shows a leaning toward North American practice.

However, unless the LNER determined to em-phasise the leap forward in styling No.10000 rep-resented, it seems curious that it should have been heading a somewhat ramshackle and ancient double running-board coach as it emerged from Leeds City Station in this historic picture. Sadly, the loco was something of an experiment which failed. Its high-pressure water tube boiler proved unsatisfactory in service and eventually the en-gine was rebuilt at Doncaster in more convention-al form. *Neg.No.211/B11*

Turning it on — the chap with the trilby hung it on the turntable railing, spat on his hands, and then threw his weight behind that of the driver and fireman to help crank round the LNER's new turntable at York. 'Pacific' No.2596 'Manna' was being used, in 1932, to demonstrate the effectiveness of the turntable in handling locomotives of this size. *Neg.No.RAIL 12*

The magnificent National Railway Museum at York had as a forerunner a tiny museum inaugurated in the 1920s by the LNER in the area of York's original station. Here, in June 1934, North Eastern Railway 'Aerolite' and London & North Western 'Columbine' are welcomed to the museum by railway VIPs. The 'Pacific' 'City of Kingston-on-Hull' just happened to be in the background but it never made it to either museum, being despatched to the great railway museum in the sky via scrapyard torches. *Neg.No.RAIL 9*

A Fishy Tale

Brian Caswell

"BURTON Salmon! Burton Salmon!" We got tired of hearing this cry echo through our house in Castleford in 1948. It issued forth from my father – 'Cornelius' to everyone – in his best town crier's voice. It went on for a whole week until the very windows rattled.

What was it all about? "Bah! Gum," Cornelius exclaimed, from behind the local paper. "Hey oop," we responded, "what's to do?"

"There's a job here right up my street,"

he said. "They're wanting a porter at Burton Salmon station. I'll write off for it right away." So he wrote off in his best Castleford script. A week later he was on his way to York by train, summoned for his medical and aptitude tests and an interview.

"Now, what colour's this, Mister Caswell?" the examiner asked, showing him a green signal lamp…

"It were a piece of cake." gabbled Cornelius to mother and me, as he rushed excitedly through the door. I've passed t'medical and tests with flying colours."

All the next week he was like a cat on hot bricks, waiting for the magic letter to arrive from British Rail. Every day he practised his porter's cry of "Burton Salmon!" He even cycled the six miles to Burton Salmon station to meet the stationmaster and make a practise call on the actual platform.

Then the fatal letter came through our letterbox. It landed with a dull thud.

It read: 'We regret to inform you that we

cannot offer you the position of porter at our Burton Salmon station. Although you passed our medical and aptitude test, it has come to our notice that prior to nationalisation, you have worked for both the LMS and LNER railways, which you failed to disclose in your letter of application. Yours faithfully, etc.'

Poor Cornelius. All that practice and anticipation for nothing. One might have felt that his past experience would have carried some weight. Perhaps it was an early symptom of the current 'you're over-experienced' syndrome.

He bore no grudge, but he never cried "Burton Salmon" again until the Beeching Axe fell on that outpost of British Railways' power.

He startled us with a sudden requiem "Fancy that," he said, "no shouts of 'Burton Salmon' ever again."

Mr Caswell lives at Banks Avenue, Pontefract

Built as a 2-8-2 for use on the steeply-graded Edinburgh-Aberdeen line, LNER Class P2 2001 'Cock O' The North' is pictured on exhibition in 1934 at its birthplace — Doncaster. It was rebuilt ten years later with a 4-6-2 'Pacific' wheel arrangement and in its later years was based at York.

Neg.No.RAIL 29

Mirror finish — a shiny 'Blue Peter' is reflected in a large puddle in the old goods yard at Wellington Street, Leeds, in June, 1971. The occasion was a weekend railway exhibition organised by Yorkshire Post Newspapers whose then new building was beyond the engine. The A2 'Pacific', built by British Railways in 1948, but livened in LNER colours for preservation, helped to attract 20,000 visitors to the weekend show. With the engine is Geoffrey Drury, a businessman who played a key role in saving this Doncaster-built loco from the scrap heap. Yes, the nameplate was missing, probably as a precaution against too-ardent enthusiasts and souvenir hunters. *Neg.No.RAIL 37*

The 'Duchess of Hamilton' (No.46229) with the 'Mail by Rail' special at Leeds City on November 11, 1980, on its way from Liverpool to York to mark the 150th anniversary of mail being carried by train. *Neg.N/A*

The Train Now Leaving

JUST as the motorways led to new markings on maps, the coming of railways soon had map lines linking hundreds of towns and villages. Yorkshire had more than many in both respects and the West Riding, particularly in the Leeds area, had a 'cat's cradle' of lines built to service the huge concentration on mines and industry in the region.

Radiating from Leeds were the lines that carried important trains whose names were known to practically every schoolboy. And such schoolboys knew on which end of every platform, which side of every bridge, which end of every tunnel and on which side of every junction were the best positions to get pictures — usually with Box Brownies — of all these nationally-famous trains; pictures that are now regularly turned out on Sunday af-

ternoons and shown to great grandsons, streetwise with computers but who would not know the front-end of the Great Western's 'King George V' from the back of a 'Black Five's' tender.

A pre-war flyer reinstated in 1948, 'The Queen of Scots' ran from King's Cross to Edinburgh via Leeds and Harrogate. 'The West Riding Limited', a new streamliner launched in 1937, ran from Leeds to London in two and three-quarter hours 'The North Briton', a daily Leeds-York-Edinburgh-Glasgow express, received its title in May 1949. 'The Devonian', a Bradford and Leeds holiday express, ran to Torquay and Paignton.

Meanwhile, the 'Thames-Clyde' express ran via Leeds and Carlisle to Glasgow (St Enoch). And there were others, some of which are pictured here.

A4 60006 'Sir Ralph Wedgewood', hauling the 10.20am Leeds to King's Cross past Copley Hill on August 2, 1952. Compare it with other A4 pictures to see how the removal of the skirting had changed its appearance — and that of other members of the class — from their streamlined heyday of the 1930s. *Neg.No.20/C652*

What Clean Air Act? The dome of Leeds Town Hall can just about seen through the murk to the right of A3 60046 'Diamond Jubilee' as it heaves 'The White Rose' express through Wortley, Leeds, on October 16, 1951. One can almost trace the line of the route by the curve of the smoke trail. Many a destroyer captain would have been envious of the efforts of the lads on the footplate in the days when smokescreens were at times an essential part of survival. How things have changed: but you have to admit this picture reeks of railway atmosphere! *Neg.No.13/C596.*

'Tea for madam? And how about you, Sir?' Obviously not the driver speaking to his mate, but there would be dozens of such polite enquiries going on back in the Pullman cars as 'The Queen of Scots' Pullman, from Glasgow to London, left Leeds with A1 60119 'Patrick Stirling' moving along nicely. Note that the engine was fitted with a flared-top chimney which replaced the earlier 'stove pipe' type; not that the modification was likely to be the main topic of conversation in any of the Pullman cars as its smoke passed over them on October 15, 1952. *Neg.No.1/C664*

The photographer made a rare catch when he spotted this train en route from Leeds to Scarborough. At its head, passing Neville Hill, is a Class B16/2. This 'typically British' engine, No.61475, was captured by the camera on November 27, 1951. *Neg.No.14/C607*

Running on lines which reflect considerable pride on the part of the 'ground staff', B1 61259 climbs out of Leeds via Killingbeck with York Road almost lost in its vapour trail. It has some interesting rolling stock in tow. *Neg.No.4/C698*

Another tribute to 'the lads' — track, engine and coaches are all in good fettle in this picture, also taken at Killingbeck, as B1 No.61216, on its way from Leeds to Hull, approaches Crossgates.*Neg.No.1/C698*

Almost the same spot, an assortment of coaches trails B1 61239 as it picks up speed with a York-bound train in the Leeds eastern suburbs. When the picture was taken, in May, 1953, one of the four signals in the foreground had still not been 'modernised' and sported an ancient slotted-post lower quadrant arm and venerable pointed finial. *Neg.No.7/C698*

A fine show of steam power from 60855, one of the 184 'Green Arrow' Class V2 locomotives, picking-up speed through Wortley, Leeds, with an express. These engines were equally at home on goods or passenger work. October 17, 1951. *Neg.No. 15/C596*

With a heavy load behind and a well-stacked tender, 'Jubilee' 45659 'Drake' pounds out of Leeds with 'The Thames-Clyde Express' from Glasgow to London. October 17, 1951. *Neg.No.10/C596*

Finally, just to switch the theme, two trains on their way *into* Leeds: V2 60865 was on its way into Leeds Central on August 1, 1952. The engine was matched with a low tender and the ex-LNER coaches are interesting. There is evidence over to the left that the railways were still heavily into the handling of goods traffic. *Neg.No.3/C651*

…and last of all, Class B16 No.61424 was hurrying through Killingbeck towards Leeds City with empty passenger stock when the photographer caught it on May 8, 1953. *Neg.No.9/C698*

On Shed

WHILST the ends of particular platforms represented an approach to heaven to many a schoolboy steam train spotter, the lad who really wanted to get into engines had only one ambition: to get 'on shed'. This expression was coined to describe the activity surrounding an engine in a locomotive depot for major or minor servicing, cleaning, 'fettling-up' or just simmering away, awaiting its next turn of duty.

Generally dominated by a coaling tower — ranging from Heath Robinson-like contraptions of strapped timbers at small sheds, to giant concrete bunkers — these areas of wheezing, puffing, snorting, simmering, clanking, whistling, smoking, steaming engines were fascinating. And dirty too.

Young lads setting out to be express engine drivers (then the equivalent of today's airline pilots) started out as cleaners, as filthy a job as can be imagined. With coal as the basic fuel, black was he predominant shade around engine sheds.

There was grease, oil, dirty water, hot and cold ashes, giant rakes and shovels. Yet those youngsters persisted; working all hours for a pittance, going on to become firemen, and then to the pinnacle — passing out as drivers.

Those dedicated characters were said to know every signal, point, sound and smell, gradient-change and curve on the lines they used regularly. Many could also be recognised (especially on the GWR) by their beer bellies cultivated in the pubs they frequented after hours spent on hot and dusty footplates.

Now but a faded memory — a huge coaling bunker dominates this view of a selection of former LMS engines at Holbeck Motive Power Depot, Leeds. *Neg.No.D711/8*

NEVILLE HILL, LEEDS: Here's another coaling plant, and here's how it operated: loaded coal wagons (like the one against the concrete bunker just in front of the engine on the right), were hauled up the side of the tower and turned over so that their coal fell into a hopper; and were then lowered back on to the lines and shunted away. Locomotives_wanting coal were moved under the tower until their tenders were positioned under the hopper which was opened to allow coal to fall into their tenders. Simple, isn't it? Here No.60539 'Bronzino' is ready to move off after being loaded — and a task faces the fireman: breaking-up that huge piece of coal, nearly as big as him, perched just above the footplate end of the tender. November 27, 1951. *Neg.No.13/C607*

NEVILLE HILL: This closer view of the bunker shows the rails which guided the huge counter-weight for the loaded wagons. Waiting for its share of coal from the tower is 'Hunt' Class D49 No.62744 'The Holderness'. November 27, 1951. *Neg.No.8/C607*

NEVILLE HILL: Also queuing for coal that November day was A3 'Pacific' No.60084 'Trigo'. Its class had 77 members. *Neg.No.16/C607*

NEVILLE HILL: Running light engine, B16 No.61478 arrives for a fettling-up job — and looks as if it's needed. November 27, 1951. *Neg.No.5/C607*

NEVILLE HILL: No.62752 'The Atherstone', (D49 'Hunt' Class); has been cleaned and serviced and is ready for action. The coach behind it — which had probably seen service as a guard's van — sprouted all manner of projections on the roof; two-level running boards on its flanks and appeared to date back to the year dot! November 27, 1951. *Neg.No.4/C607*

NEVILLE HILL: A tired-looking Class J39 No.64850 clanks slowly by, seemingly worse for wear or, as model railway buffs would have it, 'well weathered'. November 20, 1951. *Neg.No.5/C604*

COPLEY HILL, LEEDS: Class A1 No.60141 'Abbotsford', pictured with the streamlined nose of A4 'Dominion of New Zealand' just visible in the background. August 1, 1952. *Neg.No.9/C651*

COPLEY HILL: Here's a view of the coaling arrangements, with a wagon on what looks like the upper floor of a barn, and tipper barrows lined-up above the tender of A4 No.60013 'Dominion of New Zealand', carrying the nameplate of 'The White Rose' express on its nose. Even with its streamlined skirting removed, for easier maintenance, this was a fine-looking engine. August 1, 1952. *Neg.No.13/C651*

COPLEY HILL: The speedy Antipodean is lost behind its classmate — 60029 'Woodcock' — which is doing what used to cause small boys to hide behind their mothers' skirts, and grandmas to hold on to their hats — noisily ejecting steam from its cylinder draincocks. Let's hope the lads on the footplate don't move off forgetting that their billy cans of tea are resting on the fairing below the cab, or there will likely be another sound that will cause grandma to put her hands over her ears before the day is out. August 1, 1952. *Neg.No.17/C651*

COPLEY HILL: An attentive driver keeps an eye on what's going on behind as he moves his Class J50 tank — 68937. August 1, 1952. *Neg.No.6/C651*

COPLEY HILL: This emotive view looking down the yard towards Leeds city centre clearly shows where the tank engine in the previous picture had been standing, just to the right of the shed's entrance. On the left there are two ancient brake vans, and to their left what are believed to have been some 'grounded' camping coaches. Beyond them is the well-known roof of the carriage works with a mixed string of coaches lined-up alongside. It has not been possible to identify the A4 standing in the centre of the photograph. To help you find your way around the next picture, note the fence running alongside the yard just beyond the lines of open wagons at right centre. *Neg.No.C940/6*

COPLEY HILL: The fence mentioned in the last picture runs straight ahead of the boiler of B1 No.61366 heading towards Leeds in the fading sunshine of a winter's afternoon. The nose of an express engine is protruding from the entrance to the sheds, the two old brake vans are left centre (above the coaches on the passing train), what are believed to be camping coaches come next; obviously lower than carriages parked against the wall of the carriage works. Date unknown. *Neg.No.D711/9*

COPLEY HILL: Another tank — 68911 — shows up in the background as freshly painted (green) A1 No.60139 'Sea Eagle' posed before the shed entrance, the driver in a moment of quiet contemplation as his engine simmers. August, 1952. *Neg.No.21/C652*

Into The Trough At 60mph

Alan Cowlewell

IN late 1949, I transferred from Copley Hill shed, Leeds to Sowerby Bridge Motive Power Depot to become a fireman, having waited years to get my firing turns in. My first turn was on a Saturday 'B' Special. In fact it was the Players of Nottingham works outing, which required three trains on that occasion.

My mate (Tommy 'Snuffy' Simpson) and I were on Sowerby station at 11am. We relieved a Wakefield crew who got into the first compartment next to the tender. The Nottingham crew who they had relieved were already in there.

The engine was a 2-6-0 'Crab' and what coal there was in the tender was so far back I had to shovel it twice, first from the back to the footplate end, and then into the firebox. What a job! It was mainly coal 'eggs' and the infamous 'nutty slack'.

However, we set off at a fair lick and old Tom said: "We have to get a good speed with this tin can so that we can pick up water from the troughs at the other end of Sowerby Tunnel." I had never been over water troughs before, so Tommy gave me two minutes instruction. Then on reflection, he said: "I think I had better do it – you drive."

We did not know the actual speed on that engine but knew that to get a reasonable amount of water into the tender, we had to travel at over 60mph. Going at that speed, with 10 bogies (coaches) behind, it was all over the place, and I realised why drivers had nicknamed that type the 'Crab'.

We passed over the starting end of the trough at a fair lick. Tommy lowered the scoop and then, what a bang: it just sounded as if it was digging into the ballast. Suddenly, we were absolutely deluged with water. It came over the tender in great jets and flew everywhere. Later we found the lid of the tender tank had been left open so, as fast as we scooped up the water from the trough, it was shooting out of the top of the tank.

Tommy was doing his best to lift the scoop; and I was doing my best to reduce speed. We managed to get things under control and felt a bit happier.

Not so the footplate crews in the carriage compartment behind the tender. Up to the scoop being dropped, they had been enjoying a game of cards; and a bit of fresh air through the open windows. It appears that most of the water which shot out of the tender top fell back on the leading carriage and went through the open windows. They were drenched, and as we didn't stop until we got to Blackpool they were no happier to find it pouring with rain. I doubt they had a good day. Later on, Tommy and I worked the special back to Sowerby and were relieved by the (now dry) Wakefield men who in turn, were relieved by the Notts men.

So, three drivers, three firemen, one engine. Who says the railways were not economical in the old days.

Mr Cowlewell lives at Stanningley, Leeds.

BR Standard Class 2 'Mogul' No.76025 was either fresh out of Doncaster Plant Works or had been 'on shed' for a down-to-the-metal repaint job when this picture was taken. Unfortunately, we do not have the date. In fact, she was so well turned out she made the world steam record holder — 'Mallard' — standing alongside look positively dowdy. No wonder the lads on the footplate looked pleased with themselves. *Neg.No.1/534T*

There were turntables operated by electric motors with rated horse power; others were operated by vacuum power, some by simple winding gear, and in parts of the world hydraulics were tried out, but here at Leeds Central on October 17, 1951 it was one-man power that was doing the shifting. Note the carefully-angled brickwork around the turntable pit which allowed such supermen to gain added traction. Not exactly 'on shed' but worthy of inclusion in this section. *Neg.No.4/C596*

Railway Race Tracks

THE 'singing' of pantographs on overhead wires of the East Coast Main Line, and the sound of steel wheels on continuously-welded track as the smooth-sided coaches of today's electric expresses speed along, indicate a sophisticated operation compared with the exciting sound of the great steam expresses of the past.

First was the tiny plume of steam or smoke in the distance. Then came the muffled thumping along the rails from the great driving wheels of the big express engine. The noise would grow louder and finally the whole contraption hurtled past in a blur of pistons, connecting rods, steam and smoke.

There was always the unmistakable reek of a 'living' steam engine as it shook the ground on which you stood.

It was a bonus from this eruption of engineering magnificence if the driver should happen to blow the whistle as he roared past. If it was one of the neck-tingling chime whistles of a streamlined A4, going full out, then your day was well and truly made.

Here is a selection of express engines on some of Yorkshire's long straights — the 'race tracks' of the railway world.

The station at Sessay, North Yorkshire, vibrates to the passing of V2 No.60974 with an express on the famed fast stretch between York and Darlington. *Neg.No.1/C683*

'Gentlemen' it says on the sign on Sessay's platform as A2 No.60533 'Happy Knight' races through, hopefully toward a shed where it could be given a good clean. Below the sign stands a lone railway employee, the only human in sight. Which leads one to wonder what facilities there were for any lady who ventured to de-train out here in the wide-open spaces of North Yorkshire. February 13, 1953. *Neg.No.5/C683*

At speed four miles south of Thirsk, A2/2 No.60502 'Earl Marischal' with a Newcastle-Bristol express. February 13, 1953. *Neg.No.4/C683*

Heading the other way, Edinburgh-bound A1 'Pacific' 60144 'King's Courier' accelerates northwards from York in March, 1956. *Neg.No.C927/3*

...and shortly afterwards is followed by one of the last locomotives to be built at Doncaster for the LNER, A2/3 No.60522 'Straight Deal'. *Neg.No.C927/2*

British Railways had been nationalised five months when this view was taken in May, 1948, of V2 No.976 (it still carried its LNER number) as it picked-up water from the troughs at Danby Wiske, north of Northallerton. The photographer's companion is in the right foreground trying to es-cape the flying spray. Note the 'kink' in the right-hand line of the track on the right. *Neg.No.17/258C*

More kinks in the right-hand line, beyond the 'Limit of Shunt' sign, as 'Green Arrow' V2 Class No.60975 thunders under the bridge at Sessay with a Liverpool-Newcastle express on February 13, 1953. The wheelbarrow, meanwhile, seems to have been left in a rather precarious position. *Neg.No.3/C683*

Whoever was in charge of the barrow was still out of sight when, shortly afterwards, the A1 'Pacific' named 'Midlothian' appeared at the head of an ex-King's Cross express destined for Glasgow. Those A1 engines with their off-beat exhausts had a habit of creeping up on you but the barrow boy probably had ample warning to get clear beyond the bridge wall at Sessay. The train's passengers would be getting a good view of winter conditions in the Broad Acres as the train obeyed a speed re-striction on that February day but it would soon be up to express speed again, heading for its home country across the border, y'ken. *Neg.No.2/C683.*

Glorious day, glorious view. One of the LNER's A3 Class, built in Glasgow, No.60065 'Knight of This-tle', makes good time towards York on that famous four-track main line from the north on a sunny day in 1956. It is just passing the '200 miles from Edinburgh' sign, which is 'end on' on the left. The engine's name at that time was still the subject of controversy. Originally its name plates read 'Knight of the Thistle' but following a repair and maintenance visit to the shops in December, 1932, when it reappeared the word 'the' was missing from its title and this was never corrected, despite much protest.
Neg.No.C/927/4

A grand representation of railway progress across the Plain of York: A4 No.60012 'Commonwealth of Australia' leads the Edinburgh-London non-stop flier 'The Elizabethan' at Alne, in July 1959, before the four-track lines of the 'racetrack' had been completed. It is an idyllic steam age scene: the Railway Hotel slumbers on the left; sheets waft on a washing line beside behind the lineside cottages; there are hen-pens and garden sheds and, over it all no doubt, the hair-raising sound of the engine's splendid chime whistle as its driver urges it to-ward the capital city. Good on you, mate!
Neg.No.B1W52

On another fast stretch of what is now the East Coast Main Line, A2/2 No.60501 'Cock O' The North' charges along with a Colchester-York express near Doncaster. The deflector plates on each side of the chimney seem to be performing well in lifting smoke clear of the cab windows. June 26, 1952. *Neg. No. 10/C642*

Red Alert For Goods Train

J. Waters

IN my role as 'blocklad' in a very busy, one-man signal box, my job was to record in a large black ledger the times of all train movements through our section.

I was 16 years old at the time and worked with a signalman named Jim, who suffered from attacks of a bronchial nature. The first thing he did when coming on duty was to open the high sliding windows of the box. It was like working in a sanatorium, but it suited Jim. On the one hand it provided him with greater access to the vast quantities of fresh air which his lungs apparently required; on the other, in best Western saloon style, it enabled him to spit freely through the openings without worrying unduly about the need for accuracy of direction.

Jim was a big, well-built man, who always wore an open-necked shirt. His face was permanently pink and flushed. He didn't suffer fools gladly and would swear at all engine drivers who dawdled as they crossed his busy junction.

He didn't set out to educate me. He treated me as a workmate; I did my job and he did his. For instance, at the start of each night shift, he would leave me in charge of the signal box and go off and oil some nearby points, in order to make his job easier for the next eight hours.

I was left alone to work two trains. The first was a London to Leeds express. This was a straightforward affair, but the second one – a local goods train, was a bit more complicated.

On one occasion while working this train, I inadvertently 'locked' a signal lever which needed to be free to allow the train access to the next section. It was no real problem: I could have broken into the small glass case and used the key to undo my mistake.

It would have meant, of course, that my boss would find out about the clanger I had dropped. Instead, I considered Plan B which involved the highly-polished hand lamp.

Frantically waving it about, its lens in the red position, I leaned out of the window and brought the approaching goods train to a halt.

"What's up Bobby?" asked the driver.

Taking a deep breath, I calmly invited him to pass my starter signal at red.

When the implications of my message sank in, he began to get quite agitated. Drivers had a thing about passing any signal at red!

But I managed to calm him down and explain the situation. I pointed out that the next box was expecting him and that he could see their signal in the 'clear' position.

Eventually convinced, he steamed away past the offending signal in perfect safety.

Happily for all concerned, nothing more was said about the matter. What a relief.

Mr Waters lives at Swinnow Road, Leeds

Leeds Central Station

In the days of the 'railway rivals', 'railway races' and 'railway kings', much of central Leeds, particularly south of the River Aire, and a number of near and distant suburbs were a hive of railway activity.

Taken from *The Illustrated London News Social History in Victorian Britain* by Christopher Hibbet (published by Angus & Robertson), this panoramic engraving was made by an artist from an early railway bridge across the River Aire.

All the railway property in the view has long gone, with the exception one of the two stone towers which appear near the centre of the engraving, and the bridge itself. Both were retained with a view to preservation and/or refurbishment but it has not quite worked out like that; the once fine balustrades on the bridge have, in particular, suffered badly from vandalism.

The long wall (left centre) marked the boundary between Bean Ing Mill, a once-proud monument to the Industrial Revolution (now the site of the Yorkshire Post Newspapers Building), and a large railway goods yard with extensive warehouses.

The lines on the right ran down from the bridge to the Central Station, in the distance, with the Great Northern Hotel (later the Wellesley), standing prominently near the right-hand edge of the picture. All those lines and the station buildings were carried on viaducts or man-made embankments which were a tribute to the foresight, business acumen, blood and sweat of the railway planners and builders. There would probably have been tears, too, had they known that the whole lot would be torn down and removed before the end of the 1960s.

The Aireside Centre Development, Royal Mail House and the Holiday Inn Crowne Plaza now stand on land returned to the level of the water meadows where cattle had grazed alongside the river before the arrival of Benjamin Gott to erect his woollen mill at Bean Ing, in 1792, helping to propel Yorkshire into the forefront of the woollen industry.

The railway navvies had worked miracles in meeting the demands of the architects. Some of the stone work was so massive (as in Great Northern Street, near the present Royal Mail House) that demolition work was long delayed and traces of the original bridge wall remain to this day, as does a Great Northern property boundary stone in the front wall of the Wellesley Hotel.

For years locals were keen to point out the scars made by World War Two German bombs in the walls of the old goods yard offices alongside Wellington Street.

So, these few items are all that is left of a once busy station. The infamous Wellington Street wind long ago dispersed Central's famous sounds: the clank of buffers and couplers in the goods yard, the rush of exhausting steam as the wheels of commuter trains slipped whilst trying to gain a grip on wet November nights and -most missed of all — the unique sound of an A4 streamliner's chime whistle as it quickly gathered speed, its tail light reflecting on the rails, as it faded 'up Beeston' and raced towards King's Cross.

Most of the 'crack' trains from Leeds to London started from Central. The station was shared by various companies over the years, but latterly by the LNER and LMS. This picture clearly shows the ramp leading up from Wellington Street to the station car park. As recorded above, Royal Mail House now stands on this site and the third floor of today's building is positioned about where the gable ends of the train shed are on this old photograph. Judging by the style of the cars and the fact that the YMCA Forces Canteen appears to be still operating in the station building, it would seem to have been taken in the years just after World War Two. A Brylcreem poster on the hoardings features a sailor — strange, considering that RAF types were more closely associated with that product! Dalton's Cereal Flakes were still in business and some of those splendid holiday posters were starting to appear again. The Great Northern Hotel was just off to the left of the picture. *Neg.N/A*

The engine was clean, the coaches hardly so. The platform canopies certainly looked as if they had seen better days in this picture, most likely taken in the early post-war period, for B1 No.61114 wore nationalised livery, Pride in steam still meant enough to the blokes at its home shed that they could turn it out looking spick and span. *Neg.N/A*

Across Wellington Street, and easily within whistle-sound of Central Station, was Tetley's 'North Eastern' pub. Although named for one of the companies whose name was a by-word in West Yorkshire, the pub was not so much a watering hole for railwaymen (the 'West Riding' at the other end of Wellington Street was more handy for thirsty locomen) as it was for the staffs of the *Yorkshire Post* and *Yorkshire Evening Post* whose new building was less than 500 yards away. The pub's demolition was one of the fastest jobs performed in the city. Some newsmen who had been drinking there on a Friday night swore they returned to work on the Monday morning to find it flattened! Mysteriously, the then editor of the *Yorkshire Evening Post* came into possession of the only known souvenir — a brass bell which used to stand on the bar to attract the landlord's attention. Maybe his attention wandered that last night. *Neg.F240/5*

There was a stationmaster, there were signalmen, there were drivers, shunters, humble tanks and mighty express engines: but the chap of whom everybody took notice at the 'throat' of Leeds Central was the fellow adjusting the lamp on A3 No.60112 'St Simon'. Nothing missed the eagle eye of the inspector. His amply-filled uniform belied a man with some considerable agility as he performed a fine balancing act on the protective walkways above point rodding and signal wires; a nod for the well-known, a withering glance for a driver 'odding t'job up'. October 17, 1951. *Neg.No.7/C596*

…here our friend admires the power behind the regulator as the thundering exhaust shows 'St Simon's' wheels were slipping when the engine started to heave its London-bound train out of Central. *Neg.No.3/C596*

High and mighty — V2 No.60864, eager for the 'off' with a King's Cross express in July, 1959, the fireman enjoying his 'fag' before he turns his attention to the tons of coal in the tender. *Neg.No.BIW 34*

Rails everywhere — and some of them greasy; unburnt coal dust flies up to the skies as an A1 slips when starting her train. No.60125 'Scottish Union' was pictured in August, 1952. One of Gresley's fine coaches is over on the right with a closed corridor door solid enough to keep out the weather at the 'front end' and of a quality to fetch a very good price today in occasional stores that specialise in such items. *Neg.No.28/C652*

The only thing remaining in 1997 from this picture of 1951 is the stone-built tower in the background. A1 No.60123 'H.A. Ivatt', named after a locomotive designer, made a proud picture just off the end of Central's platforms. *Neg.No.9/C596*

At one time the most common-place engines in the North of England were the 'Black Fives' of the LMS. Between 1934 and 1951, some 842 were built. One of them — No.44689 — making easy work of three coaches in the two-tone livery popularly known as 'blood and custard', is pictured approaching the LMS side of Central. *Neg.No.8/C596*

Few pictures in editions of *Portraits of Steam* have attracted so many 'thank you' letters from 'average enthusiasts' than this one: here is the passenger concourse of Central Station, scene of countless happy homecomings and sad farewells. And how things have changed since its disappearance! Pointers include: an advertisement above the bookstall shows *The Lady* selling for one shilling (5p); travel — a suitcase near the centre of the picture bears a 'wanted on voyage' sticker, for the jumbo jet had not then been invented; religion — a poster tells travellers the times of masses to be held at St Anne's Cathedral and St Patrick's Church, York Road (today it is estimated that more people in the greater Chicago area go to church on Sunday than do in the whole of mainland Britain). But there was much more litter on the station then, especially near the seated passengers, than one expects to find on larger stations today. *Neg.No.P/298A*

The previous picture of Central's concourse raised so much interest, at a later date we decided to run another one — looking the other way from the corner of the bookstall and out from the platforms towards signs for Enquiries and Reservations office; 'Way Out and to City Station and Queen's Hotel — 3 minutes' (there must have been some fit folk about in those days); and the Refreshment Room. The Mount Family and Commercial Hotel, in Clarendon Road, Leeds, was advertising a room with bath and breakfast for 22s 6d; other advertisers included the Co-op 'Choose CWS and dividend', a Sanforized shirt manufacturer and — now a world away from an almost decimated Yorkshire coalfield — an advertisement for Fenaplast nylon-wefted coal conveyor belting. And if you wanted to check where it was being used, the North East and Eastern Regions of BR were advertising 'Day Line' diesel tickets 'covering the greater part of Yorkshire' for 15 shillings (75p). *Neg.N/A*

No Protest Over These 'Hunts'

"THEY were as familiar a sight as the postman," said a long-retired LNER employee, speaking of its D49 'Hunt' Class engines introduced in 1927, long before the anti-Hunt lobby or anti-train spotter brigade had been heard of. They were certainly a familiar sight on the company's Yorkshire lines.

The 'Hunts' after which they were named stretched as far apart as 'The Aberdeenshire' to 'The Cotswold', with over a dozen, including 'The Bramham Moor', 'The York and Ainsty', 'The Bedale' and 'The Badsworth' representing Yorkshire.

From 1928 onward, the D49 4-4-0 locos were developed, modified, and some rebuilt with the Lent Rotary and Oscillating Cam poppet valves being an interesting feature. Some had ex-Great Central tenders, others ex-North Eastern tenders; the rest had the LNER type. Loco weights varied between 62 and 66 tons; and tenders between 44 tons 2cwt and 52 tons. Pressure: 180lbs; Cylinders (three) 17ins x 26ins; others 20ins x 26ins. Driving wheels 6ft x 8ins. Total built: Class D49/1 — 34; Class D/49/2 — 41; Class D49/4 — 1.

Far from the huntsman's cry and the fresh countryside, 62772 'The Sinnington' was surrounded by Leeds smog at City Station in December, 1952. A nameplate from this engine was on offer at an auction of railwayana in Sheffield in April, 1994. *Neg.No.1/C674*

There was some spa town sunshine at Harrogate for 62768 'The Morpeth', based at nearby Starbeck, on November 29, 1951. The engine was unique, being classed as a D49/4 following its rebuild with two cylinders in 1942.

Neg.No.8/C608

STEAM TALES

Costly Spin On A Donkey

Dennis A. Marshall

I WAS working as an engine cleaner, aged 16, at Holbeck Loco Shed, Leeds. Occasionally we were given various other jobs to do – one of which was called 'knocking up'.

That is, to go along to a driver or fireman's house and knock on the door or window to make sure they were awake and ready to report for duty. They had to sign a slip to acknowledge our call.

On this particular night, at around 2am one of our senior cleaners was chosen to do the job.

If the call was some distance away, you could draw a rather large 'sit-up-and-beg' bicycle from the stores. This chap, however, decided to walk. We found out why later.

He was quite a joker and a bit of a fool. Some time later we had finished cleaning our first engine and, with none of us having been chosen to go out as locomotive fireman, we were hanging around, when we heard someone shouting "Tally ho!" and in came passed cleaner Cutler astride a very small donkey!

We all started shouting "Tally ho" and guided him into No 2 shed where we put him on the engine turntable and turned him round to go out again! None of noticed that while we were doing this, we were being watched by the chargehand. His remarks were as follows: "Very B***** Funny; all of you clock off and go home." We were all suspended for two days without pay!

At that time I was drawing the princely sum of £2.55 for a 48-hour week. Passed cleaner Cutler was receiving the man's labouring wage of £4.20 per week. So it turned out to be rather a costly prank!

Mr Marshall lives at Churwell, Leeds

No.62755 switches lines as it arrives at Leeds City for its next turn of duty after servicing at Neville Hill on October 8, 1951. This was 'The Bilsdale'. *Neg.No.9/C594*

The style of John Whitehead & Son's sign is far removed from what we expect today. But the typography concerning the driver of 62755 is on the loco's nameplate which he is polishing in a spell between duties at Leeds City. October 8, 1951. *Neg.No.7/C594*

What's the difference between 'The Cottesmore' (pictured) and the previous four 'Hunt' class engines? It was running into Harrogate on November 29, 1951. Answer: this one had its number on the buffer beam, the others appeared on smoke box doors, it was 62749. *Neg.No.3/C608*

With a final toot of a 'Hunt's' horn — sorry, whistle — 62727 'The Quorn' heads out of Harrogate into hunting country, with a Liverpool-Newcastle express in tow. Just ahead of it is a company sign which was well-known to Yorkshire folk. *Neg.No.6/C608*

Not Forgetting The LMS

THE WAY in which most of the pictures in this book came to be taken is explained in the write-up on the dustjacket, so it should come as no surprise to the reader that the accent throughout is on the locomotives and properties of the LNER. From Doncaster in the south, where the then Yorkshire Conservative Newspaper Co had a satellite printing works, to Darlington in the North; and from Leeds and its environs in the west to Yorkshire's east coast towns were the areas where most of the newspaper company's offices were located.

The penetration of the LMS (London Midland & Scottish Railway) into our circulation areas came main-ly from the western half of the country. Nevertheless, the unmistakable outlines of LMS locomotives and rolling stock were familiar enough, especially in the West Riding.

Some would say (the compiler of this publication among them), that the quality of LMS passenger stock on everyday trains around the area was generally believed to be superior to that of the LNER. And as for exterior looks, there seemed to be more smooth-sided coaches around on the lines of the former company than there were on the latter. They were great rivals but we don't mean to take sides; so to try and balance the book, let's put the spotlight on the LMS.

Left: Perhaps as a gesture (and not necessarily a rude one) to the LNER, the very last train to be hauled by this George Hughes Class 4-6-0 'Dreadnought' No.50455, (the last of its type) was a special between Blackpool and York. *Neg.N/A*

Below: Ancient (not quite) and modern: 4-4-0 No.41196 at the head of a train of then modern smooth-sided coaches. The engine is carrying its BR number but the tender still has LMS on its flanks. The loco had a certain style. As someone once said: "If there was an Aunt Lily of locomotives, then this was she…" In more factual terms she was a three-cylinder Compound introduced in 1924. The loco weighed 61 tons 14cwt; Pressure: 200lbs; Driving wheels: 6ft 9ins. *Neg.No.4/548R*

A predecessor of the last two engines, and shown off to better advantage. No.41080 was one of the original Midland Railway Compounds, introduced from 1905 onward. At 7ft, its driving wheels were slightly larger than those of the previous two engines. The Compounds always seemed to have an easy-running look about them. This one was resting in the autumn sun at Leeds City on October 9, 1951. *Neg.No.10/C594*

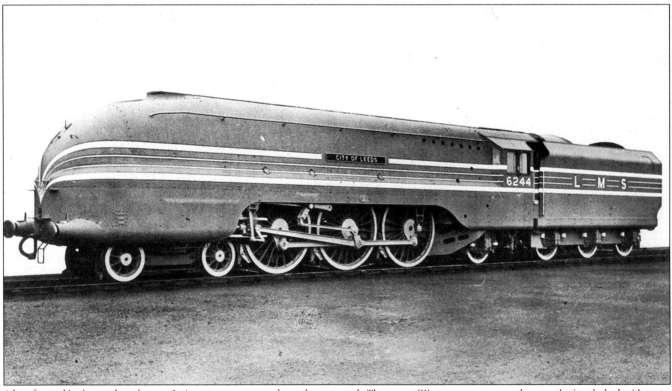

A leap forward in time, style and power. In August 1940, when Britain was getting used to the idea of 'austerity' equipment, the LMS reversed the trend and released this picture of the new No.6244 'City of Leeds' streamliner and then embarked upon a favourite railway company pastime of switching names and numbers around. The name 'King George VI' came to grace 6244 and the 'City of Leeds' name was transferred to engine 6248. Which makes this a rare picture. In common with other engines of this type, the streamlined casing was later removed for easier maintenance. In so many cases where aesthetics clashed with costs, those concerned with the latter generally came out the winners. One might well ask, why did they go to the expense of streamlining the engine in the first place? At which point most accountants would assume a blank stare. *Neg.No.RAIL 38*

When they topped-up the tenders on the LMS, they did not intend to let the lads run out of coal, as witnessed in this shot of 5704 'Leviathan'. But by the late 1940s, doubts and confusion regarding the future of nationalisation had led to a lack of attention to detail when it came to cleaning locomotives. *Neg.No.6/258C*

'Seahorse', which appears elsewhere in its BR livery, poses here in original LMS trim and number 5705. The 5XP machine has a straight-sided tender with internal 'fence' to prevent spillage of the highly-piled coal. *Neg.No.13/258C*

Many of the LMS 'Jubilees' had patriotic names, others represented heroic names as used by the Royal Navy for some of its ships. One of the latter was 5708 'Resolution' which had been 'docked' quite nicely for the photographer to get this view. *Neg.No.8/258C*

The name of this engine brings happy memories to the editor of this publication. The man who introduced him to the joys of Canadian railroads, the late Dr R.A. 'Bob' Sprenger, used to be the Canadian Government doctor in the British Columbia town which bears the same name — 'Prince Rupert'. Although in size the LMS No.5708 hardly measured up to the giant engines built to scale the gradients of the Rocky Mountains, it had similar colouring and was a fine-looking loco when turned-out in good order. The picture was taken on April 7, 1948. *Neg.No.11/258C*

Class 2MT No.46485, one of the BR-built representatives of this LMS design, entering Harrogate on November 29, 1951. *Neg.No.4/C608*

The sheer clutter of the old Leeds City Station is no better illustrated than in this October 8, 1951 picture of Class 5 No.45079 making its entry. However, photography 'buffs' didn't mind the clutter, because the angle at which daylight hit the station — when it could get in — had a way of producing some quite striking pictures. *Neg.No.4/C594*

A rather splendidly turned-out LNER coach heads up a mixed collection of rolling stock on a special from Leeds to Carlisle in July, 1959, with 'Black Five' 45329 supplying the power. *Neg.No.BIW4*

Straight and steady — a Leeds-Morecambe train at Kildwick, between Keighley and Skipton, with 'Black Five' 45040 at the head. *Neg.No.2/479R*

Gold Pass Commanded Respect

Hazel Martin

MY grandfather was a director of the Lancashire & Yorkshire Railway and my brother and I loved going on the train with him.

We would be greeted by the station master in his smart navy uniform with gold braided cap. He would salute and say "Good morning, Sir."

The porter used a trolley to take our luggage to the van, and also the mail bags and parcels, together with milk churns and various goods for stations down the line.

Then grandfather would give him a tip (worth £1 at today's values) and we were off.

When the ticket collector came round, grandfather gave him our tickets (half fare for under 14s) and showed the man his own gold pass which was attached to his watch chain.

At every station, he checked his Bradshaw railway timetable against his watch, just to make sure the train was punctual.

If it appeared to overstay its time at any station, he would question the driver when we arrived at Skipton.

The answer usually was: "We've had a lot of parcel traffic, sir," or maybe: "We had a horse box to collect."

Dad would be at the station in his Morris Oxford to collect us, then we all went home for lunch before grandfather returned on the afternoon train.

Mrs Martin lives at Bishopthorpe, York.

In 1935, No.5552, the first of the 5XP 'Jubilee' Class, was named 'Silver Jubilee' to commemorate the Jubilee of King George V. In this picture, first published in the *Yorkshire Weekly Post* on June 1 of that year, the locomotive — complete with ceremonial stainless steel fittings — is at Leeds Midland Station on the 12.42pm train to Bristol. *Neg.No.16/C593*

Dusty Answer For Lad Porter

Stanley Johnson

MY job title when I joined the LNER in the late 1940s was Lad Porter. The post, at Malton Station, North Yorkshire, covered a multitude of tasks.

First thing, before the morning mail train arrived, was to put the gas lights on.

This was achieved with a broom handle with a wire attached to permit a reach of 10 feet to the gas cock.

When the mail train arrived, I had to deal with any passengers first, then start to empty the guard's compartment of parcels, luggage, fish, letters and Post Office parcels. They had to be sorted and distributed to their respective addresses.

It was also the task of the lad porter to dust the window sills and the station seats. This was on-going, as every time a train passed they were dusted or sooted up again!

The toilets also had to be cleaned and the brass piping made to sparkle. Toilet seats, made of wood, had to be scrubbed with soap and water. When the weather was frosty, a stove had to be lit to prevent the toilets from freezing up.

At approximately 11am each day, I had to start and maintain the signal lamps. I trimmed the wicks and filled the lamps with paraffin, then climbed back up the steel ladders to polish the red, amber and green aspect lenses on the signals themselves.

There were also 'dolly lamps' to maintain (ground signals to indicate to drivers which way the points were set).

I later became a passenger shunter, then a guard, and finished my time with BR as a signalman.

I later invested £130 in my own business which was more rewarding than the railway: I now own Eden Camp Modern History Theme Museum at Malton. But I still have many happy memories of working on the railway.

Style Spans The Years

BRIDGES — be they for roads, railways or canals — have incorporated some of the great engineering feats of all time. Given considerate treatment, they can also be things of great beauty, and one of the tragedies of the most recent Balkan conflict was the near-destruction of one of the world's most picturesque bridges, apparently for no other reason than it was there.

Brunel was good at bridges and some classic examples of his work still stand with grace and style along the route of the original Great Western Railway. Stephenson's examples leaned more towards the practical than the graceful and there were other 'Brits' who put together some great spans that won the envy and respect of the world — not least the Forth Bridge; and the Sydney Harbour Bridge, 'the old coat-hanger' which carries rail tracks as well as a broad highway to the northern suburbs of the Australian city.

But when it comes to truly daring and massive bridges, the Americans and Canadians were surely out in front, putting together massive structures that ran out across the ocean for miles, whilst others clung to the sides of the Rockies and the Selkirks in Canada; and in Colorado, New Mexico and Arizona they leapt deep gorges and raging rivers.

Even the original wooden bridges, or trestles, which 'had to do' until steel replacements could be afforded or

There can be few other objects or structures in the world which have so often had their names connected with the task of painting than has the Forth Bridge. Let a friend or neighbour catch you up a ladder with a paint brush in your hand and he or she is just as likely to ask, "Is it a Forth Bridge job, then?" as they are to say, "Good morning." Generations have grown up hearing the story of how the bridge was so big that the painters started at one end and by the time they reached the other it was time to go back and start again. Unique in its shape, it rates with the Eiffel Tower and Blackpool Tower as being instantly recognisable. More recently there have been some nasty things written and said about the state of the paintwork. Perhaps it was all political, or to do with privatisation, but there were no such concerns back in September, 1936 when Doncaster-built A4 'Lord President' gave an added fillip to proud British engineering as it hauled an Aberdeen-Edinburgh express across the great span.
Picture: Fox Photos Ltd

It's a big drop in bridge size from the last picture to this one, but curiously enough this brick and stone structure probably rises higher above sea level than does the Forth Bridge. It was built to carry the Leeds-Guiseley (A65) road over the old line which ran up from the Aire Valley to Yeadon Station, not far from where Leeds and Bradford International Airport stakes its claim to be the highest civil airport in the country. At the time the picture was taken, in January, 1969, plans were afoot to turn it into a pedestrian subway. Over the years operators at the airport must have cursed the day the lines were lifted. Had they been extended to an airport station, passenger traffic would almost certainly have enjoyed the same increases as did Manchester Airport from its rail connections. *Neg.N/A*

designed in the race to link the east and west coasts of the North American continent, were often astonishing feats of construction. Latter-day engineers were full of praise for the loads which these trestles could carry, especially those that curved and climbed at the same time.

The Leeds area has its share of large bridges, but whereas it was the river which necessitated the soaring spans that pin-pointed the centre of Newcastle, it was often the very proliferation of criss-crossing railways themselves that required the rash of bridges and magnificent viaducts across all three of Yorkshire's Ridings in general and around Leeds and Bradford in particular. Here is a selection of them, although pride of place and pole position goes to the world-famous Scot...

No rail buffs they — David Banks and Joe Sutcliffe, two Bradford anglers, watched their own lines as a double-headed train passed over Arthington Viaduct, in Wharfedale, on an April day in 1976. In the lead was a 'Hardwick Precedent' Class engine built in 1892, followed by Midland Compound 1000. The two took steam enthusiasts on a run from York to Carnforth, via Harrogate and Leeds. It was organised by Gainsborough Model Railway Society and it was the first time in years that a steam locomotive had passed over this stylish structure. On the return journey, the train was hauled by the 'Flying Scotsman', due for a stay at the National Railway Museum in York. *Neg.N/A*

The steep hills and deep valleys of West Yorkshire presented a big challenge for the railway builders, but if people were prepared to build houses and mills on inclines that took the breath away, then there was no way the railway builders were going to be beaten. Typical of the many fine structures they erected was Lockwood Viaduct, Huddersfield, pictured from Hanson Lane, Lockwood in February, 1946. *Neg.N/A*

Over the top — the crew of this ex-LMS freight engine would be keeping their fingers crossed for continuing mild weather as they steamed across the viaduct carrying the Bradford-Morcambe line over the River Wenning at Clapham, three days before Christmas in 1965. *Neg.N/A*

There would be no more trains steaming over this bridge. Caught a split-second before one end hit the ground after receiving the attention of the torch-bearers, it was the end of the line for the bridge which spanned the River Ure, on the south side of Ripon Station, in April, 1972. The structure had carried the Harrogate-Northallerton line which was closed in 1969. *Neg.N/A*

Within a year of that last demolition, British Rail announced that this fine-looking structure over the River Aire at Newland, near Selby, would also come down. The 50-year-old bridge was part of the Selby-Goole line, opened in 1910 for goods traffic and opened up to passenger trains in 1912. The infamous Dr Beeching axed the line in the 1960s, but a five-mile stretch from Selby gained a temporary reprieve for goods use only, to a British Rail tip and the War Department depot at Barlow. *Neg.N/A*.

However, there were some constructive moves afoot and about the same time the demolition of the Newland bridge was being announced, in March of 1976, work was under way on this 1,000-ton steel and concrete bridge over the Leeds south-west urban motorway (M621). Train services on the Leeds-London main line were diverted as the bridge, near Elland Road football ground, was rolled into position along specially-constructed tracks. The contract for the 44-metre bridge, one of the largest single-span bridges in the country, totalled £500,000. *Neg.N/A*

Handy Solution

J.Rodley

WORKING out of Farnley sheds one afternoon in 1952, I lost the shovel off our engine's footplate whilst we were in the depths of Morley Tunnel

I then had to throw coal into the fire-box with my bare hands until we got to Hill House sheds, Huddersfield, to get a replacement!

Mr Rodley lives at Troy Rise, Morley

No trace remains of this massive piece of late 19th-century engineering that used to be a feature of south-east Leeds, other than the massive stone tower under the main section of the bridge It was built at Stourton to carry the Great Northern Railway line from Beeston Junction (near the top of Dewsbury Road, Leeds), to Hunslet East Goods Station. About that time, rumour had it that the Aire & Calder Navigation aimed to establish a form of Manchester Ship Canal linking the East Coast with Leeds. The GN, meanwhile, had planned its link line to cross the River Aire and the A & CN's canal at this point. On learning that the canal company planned to operate much taller ships, the GN decided on a swing bridge of massive proportions. The shed under the left-hand side of the bridge was, in fact, the coal staiths at the end of a line linking the canal with Waterloo Colliery. *Picture: Armley Mill Industrial Museum.*

Dry Humour Left A Bitter Taste

Dennis Marshall

COMING back from London on the Thames-Clyde Express, I was firing for a driver who was known to be rough on the regulator, and liked to see red hot cinders coming out of the chimney as fast as you could shovel coals into the fire box.

You normally shovelled a few tons of coal when running between London and Leeds, but with some drivers you never had to go into the tender. That is, when you could not reach the coal with your shovel, you had to open the double doors, then go back into the tender with your shovel and pull the coal down with your pick to make it easier to get on with the firing.

This was no mean feat when the train was moving at around 70mph. On this journey I had to go back into the tender and being still in my teens, I was pretty tired by then.

However, when we were approaching Leeds City Station, where we would be relieved by a crew from Holbeck Loco Shed, I was surprised when the driver, who had a very deep voice, asked: "Do you drink, young man?" In fact, I was so surprised I said "Yes".

"Then when we are relieved we will go into the station bar and have a pint," he said.

My spirits were lifted and when we got to the station I wiped my face with a clean rag and off we went to the bar.

In a loud voice the driver called to the lady who was serving: "Two pints of bitter, please." I waited in anticipation.

Arthur (I won't identify him beyond that), picked up the first pint she put on the counter and downed it in one swallow.

Then, picking up the second pint, he looked at me and said: "Are you not drinking then, young man?"

As my worldly wealth at that moment was one shilling (five pence today), I declined and walked back to sign off – a much wiser and very disappointed young man.

Mr Marshall lives at Churwell, Leeds.

Here are all three spans of the bridge with the huge 'swing' section on the right. In the foreground was the BR Staff Association sports field, now lost under several 'storeys' of containers. What happened to the old Gresley LNER coach (middle right), once used as a team changing room, is not known. *Picture: Peter Rose.*

And here's a close-up of the north end of the main span — and the buttress built at the end of the last century which, it is alleged, helped cause the bridge to become a 'folly'. The story has it that the bridge was opened for a test swing, but when it was swung back to line up with the rail lines, the end of the span had dropped by some 2ft and had to be jacked-up to align with the railway lines again. As if that wasn't enough, the Aire & Calder dropped its grand canal plan and tall ships never got any further inland than Goole. Consequently, the rail bridge was anchored in the closed position and never operated again. To add insult the injury, the canal company, reputed to have an intense dislike of railway competition, built its new lock almost under the bridge for its canal section which ran up to Leeds. *Picture: Peter Rose.*

This section started with one of the world's most famous bridges; it ends with a viaduct which, certainly in the last 20 years, has received almost as much publicity as the Forth Bridge. In that process Ribblehead Viaduct has been photographed countless times, but Gary Longbottom, a *Yorkshire* *Post* photographer, chose an angle which clearly illustrates the harsh terrain which had to be overcome by the builders of the Settle-Carlisle line. Here's where this tribute to the railway builders' skills meets the great slope that originally cut off the northern side of the valley; the first seven of some two dozen arches giving a cathedral-like quality to the picture as the autumn sun filters through them. A successful and much publicised campaign in the 1980s saw the line kept open and the viaduct retained. *Neg.N/A*

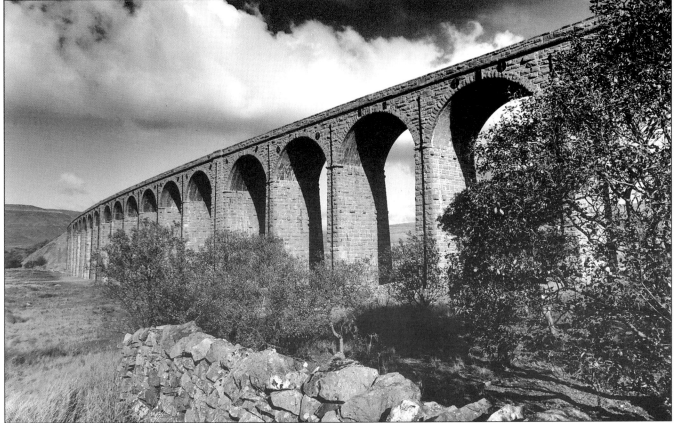

The gentle curve of the longest viaduct on the Settle-Carlisle line leads the eye once more into those mighty northern hills, and the dry stone wall in the foreground acts as a signature to the fact that this great structure stands in the Dales; and very well, too, on such a glorious day. It cost £3.5 million to renovate but countless country lovers, whether they be from Canada, Australia, Kenya, or just plain but pleasant Horton in Ribblesdale, will testify that it was money well spent.
Picture: Gary Longbottom.

Proud To Be British

SINCE it became fashionable to speak of 'designer stubble' 'designer suits' 'designer cocktails' and, would you believe, 'designer hairs of the dog', the LNER's A1 Class of locomotives have gained the description of 'designer engines' in some corners of the railway world.

Perhaps it is because at one and the same time they look beautifully British but have a certain foreign flair: the V-shaped cab front had a look of some French express engines; the 'squared-off' running boards had, some felt, a touch of North American practice about them; and anyone familiar with Australia's most famous class of Pacifics will detect a distinct resemblance Whatever the case, the

A1s had what some call 'sophisticated clout' about them and they certainty looked as if they were going places

They carried their 'modern' look right to the end of mainline steam in Britain. But whatever people said about their looks, they made small boy enthusiasts proud to be British.

CLASS A1 — wheel arrangement 4-6-2. A1/1 introduced 1945. Thompson rebuild of A10. A1 was development of A1/1 for new construction. Weights: Engine 101 tons ('Great Northern'); others 104 tons 2cwt; Tender 60 tons 7cwt. Pressure: 250lbs. Cylinders — three 19ins x 26ins. Driving wheels — 6ft 8ins.

Among the engines which carried designers' names was A1 60126 'Sir Vincent Raven', pictured here at Neville Hill, Leeds. Looking beyond it, heaven help any grime-coated would-be fireman or driver who asked the shop foreman the time. *Neg.No.1/C607*

Looking as if it was eager to be off, 60139 'Sea Eagle' was well and truly spruced-up at Copley Hill Shed, Leeds, on August 2, 1952. But even in those days, it seems, people forgot to put back the protective cover over the wiring box of lamp standards — note the one on the right. *Neg.No.22/C652*

In early BR days, various liveries were tried on locomotives; one or two were quite hideous and did not last long. However, 60134 ''Foxhunter'' was resplendent in a coat of acceptable blue when photographed near Copley Hill in 1951. Later, green was adopted as the standard colour for this type of engine. One wonders what might have happened had this name been applied to an engine in these days of political correctness.One thing is certain, protesters would have been very wary of trying to stop it. *Neg.No.1/C605*

The name of 60141 'Abbotsford' sticks in the mind of the compiler of this book more even than some of the world-famous engines which are featured. Perhaps it was that when he was using trains a lot, this engine, more than any other, seemed to be at the front end and it takes little imagination to recall the sound of its slightly off-beat exhaust when it was working up to speed. Here she is at Copley Hill, with the streamlined nose of A4 60013 'Dominion of New Zealand' just getting into the picture on the right. *Neg.No.9/C651*

'Peregrine', a name originally gracing the A4 which became 'Lord Faringdon', was revived in 1949 and given to this A1 — 60146. The driver eyes the photographer as she moves out of Doncaster with an express for King's Cross. March 27, 1952. *Neg.No.23/C625*

Proud maybe — but not snobbish — although they were intended for express passenger work, the A1s took their share of other duties. This lightweight stopping train of non-corridor coaches was a far cry from 'The Flying Scotsman' but the passengers in this mixed bag of vehicles, even if they were not steam enthusiasts, would notice a big difference in acceleration when 60120 'Kitti-wake' got into her stride. October 15, 1952. *Neg.No.2/C664*

'Out the road', the A1s took anything in their stride. In 1953 — Coronation year — 60145 'St Mungo' was belting through Otterington, between Thirsk and Northallerton, with 'The Flying Scotsman' train whose coaches still proudly wore that name and/or destination boards. *Neg.No.2/402T*

Heavy Haulers

The first picture in this section (*Neg.No.C/927/1*) is of B1 No.61273, a comparatively modest engine, heading a long goods train south across the Plain of York and it reflects the good and sad times alike of British railways. Immediately behind the tender are three distinctive high-sided coke wagons reflecting the days when coal was king. Trailing behind them, clanking and swaying, are some 40 freight wagons and vans carrying a mixed cargo of timber, coal, steel sheet, perishables, chemical drums and what-have-you. A real 'mixed manifest' as an American railroader would put it.

Such trains had become increasingly rare, even across the Atlantic, as massive 'unit trains' and 'piggyback' trailer trains equipped to specialise in one type of product — coal, oil, woodchips, grain or articulated road trailers — became more popular. Whilst the rail freight business in both America and Canada is expanding (and 'Down Under' Australian railways are going all-out to attract more freight) in Britain such trains seem to get shorter and fewer whether they be mixed goods or 'merry-go round' specials. Whilst the hassle continues regarding 'privatisation' and 'franchises', politicians who become instant experts on any subject the minute they are moved from one department to another, seem to have near overlooked the sad state of the freight business. It is quite a remarkable situation, considering their constant pronouncements about Britain's export successes, also bearing in mind that Britain's railway system as a whole has links with the Channel Tunnel, not just lines in the South East. It would take at least 20 large lorries to carry the loads hauled by the single B1 locomotive pictured below. They would fill one lane of almost the entire length of Wellington Street, Leeds: a lesson yet to be learned by those who, like TV news media, only appear to be interested in 'the environment' when some man-made disaster strikes. But the following week it is all forgotten as they move on to yet another war or famine.

The 'road lobby', meanwhile, continues to push the 'convenience' of door-to-door service which requires no railway sidings or transfers. What they fail to highlight is the astronomical costs to British companies caused by near-jammed motorways and — already here — gridlocked towns and cities.

Having experienced all those horrors, the 'can-do' Americans are doing and container-borne and piggy-back freights, moving at more than 70mph on well-maintained track, with preference given to 'hot-shot' freight trains, is showing the way head. And one rapid growth area is on 'short-haul' runs of up to 200 miles.

On the same stretch of line as the engine in the previous picture, is a south-bound former War Department 'Austerity' which drifts along at just less than the speed of the following wind, judging by the exhaust. But 2-8-0 No.90603 is packing some tonnage on a mixed goods. December 6, 1955. *Neg.No.C886/8*

Three months later, V2 No.60833 was rattling a rake of mineral wagons south on another stretch of the 'Racetrack' section north of York. Known as 'Green Arrows' after the first member of the class to appear in 1936, the V2s could turn a wheel to anything. *Neg.No.C927/5*

The flatlands around Doncaster were ideal running country for the big haulers: here's another V2 — 60876 — bowling a fast goods through Arksey. *Neg.No.8/C642*

Class 02 2-8-0 No.63956 with 43 wagons of coal, running tender first north of Doncaster. June 25, 1952. *Neg.No.6/C642*

Class 8F 2-8-0 No.48158 at Wortley, Leeds, on October 4, 1951, with a snow plough attachment remarkably like those fitted to some North American diesel types. Several engines of the 8F type served abroad during World War Two. *Neg.No.14/C593*

Introduced in 1935, Class 8F freight locomotives were real workhorses and were so successful during World War Two they were built by four other companies in addition to the LMS, and gained the nickname 'war winners'. A total of 624 was built. This one was an ex-LNER Class 06 on loan to and re-numbered by the LMS in 1947. *Neg.No.7/258C*

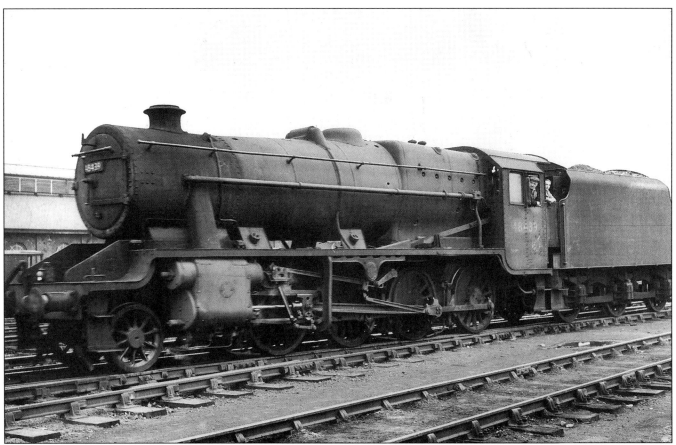

Looking as if it might well have done war service in the Middle East and finally 'returned to sender', another Class 8 — No.48439 — was at Stourton in this 1952 picture. *Neg.No.4/C649*

So you take a boiler, put a chimney on it, stick a fire box at the back and some wheels underneath and - hey presto — you've got a railway engine. Simple, isn't it? And there could have been few engines around which looked more simple and straightforward — although not necessarily more ugly — than this Class 7F 0-8-0 of the LMS. Dating back to 1929, the engines weighed 60 tons 15cwt; Pressure was 200lbs; Cylinders 19ins x 26ins driving wheels of 4ft 8ins. The small driving wheels were to make starting with heavy loads easier. A total of 175 was built. Such engines were a familiar sight on lines through the Heavy Woollen District. Pictured in March, 1948, No.9641 carried the letter 'M' above its cabside LMS number — a temporary arrangement before the figure 4 was prefixed to that number by British Railways. *Neg.No.10/258C*

A Long Rest In Bed With A Warming Brick

John Weston

MANY older readers will remember railwaymen's 'lodging turns' of duty. Driver, fireman and guard would work a train out from their home station, book off at the arrival point then go to either a railway barracks or a private house. Such workings were a common feature at most depots before nationalisation. Working out of Derby, we had a number of turns which took us into Yorkshire. Canklow, Normanton and Stourton were regular ports of call.

In 1940, while I was still a passed cleaner, or spare fireman, we lodged in Holbeck for a time. The barracks there was in the locomotive yard and trying to sleep in the daytime was no easy matter. (Most of the goods and parcel trains ran during the night and sleeping in the daytime was regarded as a normal part of the job.)

In 1941 I became a regular fireman and in March 1942, was booked into one of three North Road goods links we had at Derby. My driver, Bill Beardsley, had been in the link for 15 years or so. I shall always

associate lodging at Canklow with the Yorkshire version of the hot water bottle. A clay brick, warmed overnight in the oven, gave out a steady heat. Tired and dirty after the overnight journey, it was a case of a quick wash and then a day in bed with the gradually cooling brick.

Yet we were only 36 miles from home – the shortest regular 'overnight' run from Derby.

It only lasted until March 1943, for me then I was moved into the Wellingborough Link.

It took all of 18 years as a cleaner and fireman before I became a driver. Nowadays, a lot of people want everything tomorrow.

Mr Weston lives at Breedon-on-the-Hill, near Derby

'A machination of machinery' was how one learned driver described the ungainly appearance of these LMS 2-6-0s, best-known to most by their nickname of 'Crab'. Most footplate crews felt they were rough riders, but the curious arrangement of the inclined cylinders and associated running gear made them popular with fans who 'liked to see things whirling around'. At home with passenger or goods trains, they were something of a 'one off', although there were some LMS tank engines with a similar cylinder arrangement. One thing is certain: this one badly needed some elbow grease applying in the cleaning department.
Neg.No.9/258C

Road Sense

Ray Hemsley

THERE was once a platelayer at Ardsley who decided he would transfer to the traffic grades and get a job as a guard.

After passing out on his rules and regulations test, he was put forward for road learning.

The list clerk was surprised when he simply signed all the routes in the area and when he questioned the chap he replied: "I should know them by now – I re-laid them all!"

Mr Hemsley lives at Bruntcliffe Lane, Morley

It is surprising that the World War Two 'Austerity' engines did not get nicknamed 'Yanks'. For with that high-perched cab, Canadian-style tender, a somewhat brute force look and outside plumbing, they had a definite 'Yankee' air and the long freight trains they hauled added to the effect. Here's 90059 (centre) at York Motive Power Depot, now the site of the National Railway Museum. On the left is a more typically British Class B16 4-6-0 No.61477. *Neg.No.8/C677*

How are the mighty fallen... we take a final look at 'Heavy Haulers' and 'Austerity' engines via the one that got away; trams were stopped and other traffic had to be diverted when this one ran away backwards and crashed through a boundary wall at Marsh Lane Sidings, Leeds, on the York Road side of the main Leeds-York line. The tender came off best, the locomotive being badly damaged. It was suspected that the locomotive had been deliberately set in motion but this was not confirmed. Neg.No.225797/2

Travelling In Style

PERHAPS because some of Sir Nigel Gresley's A4 streamlined Pacifics far outlasted the streamlined coaches some of them were designed to haul, records regarding the former generally outweigh the latter. As a result, the countless thousands who have gawped at 'Mallard' or sighed over the sight and sound of 'Sir Nigel Gresley' must include a large number of people who never saw or possibly never even knew, of the then famous LNER 'Silver Jubilee' trains.

Construction began in 1935 and although below the surface the coaches followed standard LNER practice, the exteriors came with stainless steel panels covered with silver-grey rexine. Rubber sheeting concealed the gaps between coaches and stainless steel 'curtains' covered the gaps between the bogies.

The original seven coaches of each train were finished in silver-grey and comprised a twin articulated brake third, a triplet set with a restaurant car in the centre and two rear coaches — a First and a Third on twin articulated bogies.

Each train had a tare weight of 220 tons and seating was just short of 200 passengers. There was a supplementary charge for all passengers — even railway 'brass' with free tickets.

The coaches had double-glazed windows and pressure ventilation and heating. First-class compartments were

The amount of land acquired by the railway companies is no better illustrated than in this aerial picture of an unidentified A4 'Pacific' hauling one of the new Gresley streamline trains — believed to be a 'Coronation' set. When this picture was originally published in *Portraits of Steam* there was some argument as to the exact location. The editor held that the clue lay in the advertisement hoarding in the field to the left of the train: it was for the *Yorkshire Evening Post*, which, at that time, had a South Yorkshire edition printed at Doncaster. As we expected, ex-locomen and others 'bit' at the 'exact location unknown' statement and the weight of the response from them was that the train was photographed just north of Rossington, between Loversall and the Black Carr Junction. 'The train is travelling north on the Great Northern [as was] main line approaching Doncaster. The other two single lines form the end of the Dearn Valley line which extended from Edlington to connect with the GN via a flying junction at Loversall Carr', wrote Mr Ron Prattley, of Kingsley Drive, Harrogate.

He added that he had examined the layouts for all the flying junctions on the Yorkshire section of the East Coast Main Line and this was the only one to 'fit' the picture. A strong note of authority came with the plan he enclosed. *Neg.No.332D*

decorated in blue with light blue ceilings and chromium-plated fittings. Third-class coach interiors were finished in green with plated fittings.

The trains were enormously popular and by 1938 an additional third-class coach had been added to each one to increase passenger capacity to 233. Although similar externally, the coaches for the later 'Coronation' trains of 1937 saw sweeping changes in internal designs and fittings.

Gresley decided against restaurant cars, intending that meals should be served from two kitchens in each set direct to passengers at their normal places.

An employee at the Doncaster Plant Works came up with an idea for swivelling chairs at cut-away tables to facilitate this practice and Gresley agreed.

The 'Coronation' trains usually comprised four twin-articulated coaches: a brake-third, open-third, kitchen-third, open-third, two open-firsts, kitchen-third and brake-third, giving seating for 48 first-class and 168 third-class passengers.

But the big attraction was the 'beaver-tailed' observation cars attached to the rear of each train in the summer months.

Closely resembling the Bugatti railcar of the period, the tails of these cars were glass-panelled to allow an all-round view for the 16 passengers who were seated in armchairs. This, plus the efforts of the LMS, was about as near as British trains ever got to the standards which applied on North America's Santa Fe, Union Pacific, Milwaukee Road and Canadian Pacific streamliners and the then 'modern' British trains were regarded with pride by all concerned.

In 1937 the importance of Yorkshire in general and West Riding industry and commerce in particular was marked by the building of two sets of four pairs of twin-articulated coaches for the 'West Riding Limited' train for the Leeds-London service. It had the same capacity as the 'Coronation' trains and the finish was similar to that of the 'Coronation' stock, although no observation car was attached. Perhaps escaping 'Tykes' wanted no final backward glances as their train snaked up through Beeston on its way to the bright lights of London.

The 'West Riding Limited's' coaches survived for some considerable time, and some cars are believed to have been included in trains of more conventional stock.

But no less next best were Gresley's A4 Pacific engines, some of which had hauled those famous trains and steamed on to the end of an era — as pictured here.

There are those of us who would say that if you haven't heard an A4's chime whistle when it's running at speed, then you haven't lived...

It certainly made your hair curl.

The locomotive in the aerial picture was almost certainly this one: No.4489, although the nameplate had been blanked off for this test run. It was on a preliminary outing from Doncaster in 1937 with coaches of the new 'Coronation' train. Originally, 4489 carried the name 'Woodcock', but careful examination of the picture shows that the blanked-off nameplate is much too long for that name. And on the side of the cab, below the engine number, is the Canadian coat-of-arms. *Neg.No.741/W/2*

Confirmation that the train shown in the first picture of this section was in South Yorkshire came
with the unearthing of this one; the photographer's accompanying caption states that it was at
Rossington. It certainly gleamed from end to end.
The nameplate *was* a long one and, yes, there is a
coat-of-arms below the cab number. But what
name did it carry? *Neg.No.RAIL 1*

All is revealed: here in all its glory is the 'Dominion of Canada' after the official naming ceremony
carried out by the High Commissioner for Canada
in 1937. Later it was fitted with a Canadian-style
locomotive bell presented by the Canadian Pacific
Railway, and, with this attachment, left the Doncaster Plant Works in March, 1938.
Neg.No.RAIL 31

Thanks to the habit of the LNER (and other members of 'the Big Four' railway companies), of swapping engine and class numbers around for all manner of reasons, (their zeal in this respect has been exceeded by aircraft and (jet) engine manufacturers), the editor found a controversy on his hands when this picture was published in the Autumn 1995 issue of *Portraits of Steam*. One reader went so far as to suggest that the picture had been 'doctored' or was an April Fool joke played on the photographer because either the name, or number, was incorrect. 'Great Snipe' was numbered 4462, he maintained.

The editor unleashed his favourite rottweiler to sniff out the facts and he came back with this: "I quote verbatim from the RCTS book *Locomotives of the LNER Part One* (which is generally acknowledge as the standard work):

"No.4495 was painted green and named 'Great Snipe when it came out new on August 28, 1937. It went back into the paint shop on September 12 and re-appeared six days later painted blue and nameless. During the following week, 'Golden Fleece' nameplates were put on to the engine without any ceremony."

Meanwhile… "No.4462 was outshopped from Doncaster in November, 1937, and was named — you guessed it — 'Great Snipe' which it carried until July, 1941, when it was re-

named 'William Whitelaw'. No.4496 was outshopped in September, 1937, carrying the name 'Golden Shuttle' but was renamed 'Dwight D. Eisenhower' in September, 1945. The names 'Golden Fleece' and 'Golden Shuttle' were chosen as being suggestive of the woollen trade as the engines were to work the high-speed 'West Riding Limited' train."

What seems to be clear is that the photographer who took the picture below must have

snapped 4495 in that two-week period in late August/early September 1937 when it briefly appeared as 'Great Snipe' which makes the picture rare, if not unique!

We can the imagine what the lads in the Doncaster Plant Works paint shop must have been muttering about 'them as can't make their minds up about which number they want on which engine and when…'

Neg.No.RAIL 17

'Silver Fox' on the run with a moderately heavy train which made up 'The Elizabethan', on the fast 'racetrack' stretch north of York. This train made a non-stop run over the 393 miles between Edinburgh and London and the sight of the stainless steel fox which adorned the A4's flank was always a treat for train spotters. It looked much better than some of the convoluted nameplates-cum-logos which did not exactly enhance the sides of some latter-day diesels.
Neg.No.1/402T

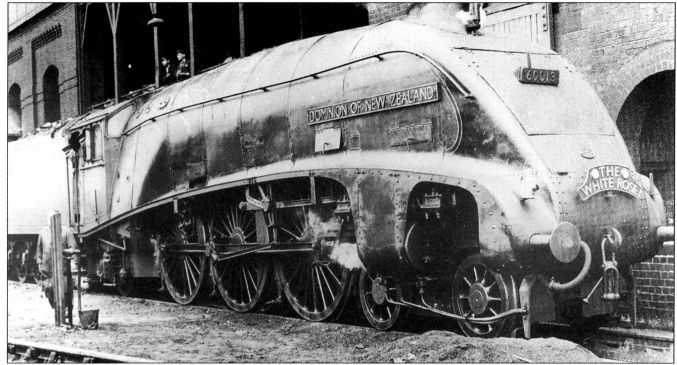

Bearing the nameplate of Yorkshire's pride - 'The White Rose' — an engine with a name from 12,000 miles away — A4 Pacific 'Dominion of New Zealand' was at Copley Hill coaling plant in 1952, being prepared for its next turn of duty. (Also see the 'On Shed' section of this book). The streamlined cladding had been removed to allow easier maintenance but the loco still had that touch of Gresley class. *Neg.No.14/C651*

STEAM TALES

Setting Store By The Good Old Days

Reg Newton

TAP, TAP, TAP – the small hours' sound of the caller-up's metal-tipped pole knocking on the front bedroom window of our end terrace house, adjoining the Doncaster Carr Loco complex, is one of my earliest memories of the late 1920s.

My father, Len Newton, was at that time a spare fireman, later to become a main line driver, with the LNER. As locomen on the day shift had to sign on very early, the company would send light-duty men or spare cleaners to 'knock-up' the footplate men.

The street was only about 100 yards from where what is now known as the East Coast Main Line passed through Doncaster. The houses, now demolished, were all gas-lit. Consequently, long before we actually heard it, we always knew of the approach of a speeding night express because the glowing gas mantle above the living room fireplace would start to flicker and tremble.

As the trains passed the house, the vibrations shook the whole place and often resulted in the complete collapse of the gas mantle!

Later on we moved to one of Doncaster's outer suburbs and in the early 1930s my father would take me with him down to the Carr Loco Sheds to collect his wages.

The area surrounding the sheds comprised rows of smoked-blackened Victorian terraced houses and I vividly remember old ladies dressed in black bombazine, fronted with hessian aprons, who on fine summer evenings sat outside their front doors smoking clay pipes.

Halfway down the street leading to the 'Loco' was George Murgatroyd's general store, where most of the railwaymen called for cigarettes and a natter. The shop was crammed from floor to ceiling with every kind of commodity. The ceiling was garlanded with whole hams and rolls of bacon, mixed among broom heads, scrubbing brushes and other items.

There was always a pleasant aroma, emanating from the sweet-smelling sawdust that covered the scrubbed floorboards mixing with the fragrance of ripe cheeses, barrelled butter and freshly-baked bread. Mint humbugs, aniseed balls and yeast made their own contribution.

At the Shed, steam engines were made ready for 'the road' (locomen hardly ever spoke of lines, rails or tracks). The locomotives ran in size from humble yard shunters to glamourous 'Pacifics' such as 'Silver Link' and 'Mallard'.

It seemed somewhat indecorous to see these grand dames of the rails in a state of undress, their smoke box doors wide open, with cleaners and oilers swarming all over them.

We would enter the timekeeper's office where a strong smell of copper penetrated all the mixture of aromas. It came from a huge wickerwork basket containing dozens of small, gleaming copper barrels. The men collected their pay in these and when they had extracted and checked the cash, they threw the 'empties' into the basket.

As a small, impressionable lad, I felt these men had the stature of rotund giants; with the scaled-down girths of the giants they controlled. And they had tongue-rolling names such as Noel Faulkner, Tommy Watchorn, Bill and Ben Barringer, Ernie Flannagan, and so on.

Most of them survived the steam age and spent happy years in retirement.

Mr Newton lives at Elmham Road, Cantley, Doncaster

Hunslet Lane Yard

THE face of Britain, more particularly many of its towns, cities, and mining areas, was scarred for years — and still is in some areas — with the remains of great industries hit by recessions, 'changes in direction' and 'reversal to core activities'.

In the light of more recent events, people tend to forget that the railway industry itself has suffered greatly, and not just at the hands of the infamous Doctor Beeching who, in fairness, was to some extent 'under starter's orders'.

The railways were among the biggest property owners in the country and great swathes of weed-strewn land across the country were evidence for years of where their core activities had once been located.

One such site was the huge Hunslet Lane Yard, not all that far from Leeds city centre, and an excellent article by Peter Rose, illustrated with his own pictures appeared in the Summer 1996 edition of *Portraits of Steam*.. No better illustration could be given of what the railways have lost. We reproduce extracts from his article here, along with some of his pictures. We also add a panoramic view of our own, specially taken to illustrate the 'before and after' effects of changing times.

Peter recalls that Hunslet Lane Yard started life as the northern passenger and goods terminus of the North Midland Railway, opened in 1840. Much of the civil engi-neering and the buildings were original. The layout altered little when passenger trains were transferred to Leeds Wellington Station in 1847.

By rail, the yard was approached from the main line at Hunslet Goods Junction. There was a single trailing connection off the 'Up' Goods Line which fanned out to the original four tracks of the North Midland Railway. These passed through a large cutting, lined with substantial stone walls penetrating several inner city suburbs before spreading out into the full width of the yard.

On the west side there were connections to Meadow Lane Gasworks and to private premises. To the east there was access via a turntable to Stewarts & Lloyds, John Fowler's and other private sidings. The Agent at Hunslet Lane was also responsible for railway traffic at the the Hunslet Engine Company and Hudswell Clarke private siding.

Having started work in the footplate grade at Holbeck Shed in October, 1950, Peter's first introduction to 'The Yard' came on Thursday, April 5, 1951 — it was his 18th firing turn. He describes work in the goods yard as being very noisy with up to three shunting engines working in close proximity, constantly moving in and out of the cutting. The regular Holbeck Shed engines at 'The Lane' were LMS Nos. 7418, 7420, and 7436, all of which took a '7' prefix under BR numbering.

Grand Day Out At The Races

Eric Drummond

'EXCURSION' – the word conjures up trips to the seaside for all the family, armed with buckets and spades, and the porter at Leeds City Station shouting: "Over the bridge for Scarborough."

But there were other types of excursion, and I well remember one of them.

The Aintree Excursion for the Grand National comprised a train of eight bogie coaches – all restaurant cars – and all carrying first-class passengers.

The train started at Newcastle and was due to change engines at Leeds. It was guaranteed to arrive on time and, in fact, was insured against late arrival.

Being first class, it had to have a first-class engine, usually a 'Black Five' which was selected some weeks beforehand and kept in Farnley Shed for special preparation, including a boiler wash-out, tubing, new fire bars and brick arch. Meanwhile, the exterior of the boiler casing, tender, etc, was cleaned several times to bring it up to ex-works standard.

The tender was swept clean of 'slack' coal and dust, then hand-filled with best steam coal. To complete the treatment, new headlamps (white), new coal pick, new firing shovel and firing irons were provided. And for the crew there were new overalls and caps.

On this particular occasion, the driver was Jack Hardcastle and I was the fireman. Because it was classed as a 'special' train, locomotive inspector 'Ginger' Wilson rode on the footplate with us to see everything went according to the rule book.

I recall that the engine's performance was excellent and it was a good 'excursion' for all concerned.

Mr Drummond lives at Syke Lane, Scarcroft. He spent 22 years on the railways, starting at Copley Hill as a cleaner and ending as a driver at Holbeck

'The Lane' was connected with the original North Midland Railway (later part of the LMS system) via this cutting. It still exists although the tracks were lifted years ago. This view is looking away from 'The Lane' and the bridge in the immediate foreground still stands, with a wire fence closing-off access to the cutting.
Neg.N/A

And this was the grand entrance to 'The Yard' from the other side of that bridge. The signal box on the left is long gone and today the back wall of the Children's World toy store, based in the Crown Point Retail Park which replaced Hunslet Lane Yard, blocks any view under the bridge from the position where the picture was taken. However, thanks to Peter Rose, we can reveal over the page what you would have seen 50 years ago when you went under that bridge.
Neg.N/A

Hunslet Lane Ya

THEN

Above: The size and importance of 'The Lane' can be appreciated in this historic photograph taken by Peter Rose. The wagons full of pre-fabricated building materials in the foreground were a part of the train shown coming through the cutting from Hunslet in the first picture in this section. The 'shed' on top of the gantry toward the left of the picture houses machinery for the rudimentary container base at that side of the yard, with several small containers clearly visible on flatbed wagons.

Only two road vehicles — actually one is a scooter, the other a lorry trailer — appear on the picture above. Now look at the contrast with the picture below which was taken in 1996 from almost exactly the same position as the 50-year-old view above.

Neg.N/A

NOW

rd in all its glory

Below: It might look more like Hackensack, New Jersey, than Hunslet, but yes, this was once Hunslet Lane Yard. Not a cinder, not a lump of coal, not a single clank of loose-coupled wagons, not a whistle, nor a snort of steam. But look back at the top picture and you can almost believe that people bundling shopping into their cars at Crown Point swear they have heard steam trains in the night; and it is on record that one person definitely saw a ghostly footplate crew. Perhaps Peter Rose should go back and shoot a few midnight shots in the empty car park and see what he comes up with…Whoooooeeee! *Neg.N/A*

Tanks For The Memory

IT WAS the sight of some particularly well-modelled LNER tank engines at the annual Normanton and Pontefact Railway Modellers' Society show that triggered the idea for the pictures in this section.

Although tank engines, real or modelled, are hardly likely to replace A4 'Pacifics' and other express engines of like size in their appeal to enthusiasts of all ages, constraints on household space and ready cash have meant that, over the years, 'starter sets' of model trains (which have put many an enthusiast under 'starter's orders'), have often relied on a tank engine as a source of power.

Not that they were all simple 0-4-0 jobs with two four-wheel coaches or wagons. Hornby had some splendid 4-4 '0' gauge tanks dating back to clockwork days, and 00-gauge three-rail manufacturers were not slow to introduce larger model tanks into their catalogues.

Perhaps their appeal as models had a connection with the appeal of the real thing: tanks could run in either direction without looking out of place; and they did away with the need for a turntable.

They found particular favour on suburban lines, where speedy acceleration, fast-running and good all-round visibility all helped to maintain schedules. (Some purists with US leanings might argue that the Pennsylvania Railroad's suburban 4-4-2s, which would no doubt have been nicknamed 'Pocket Rockets' in today's parlance, had pride of place in the fast take-off stakes). And various types of American 'Camelbacks', despite their ungainly looks, were no slouches in action on such lines.

But the good old Yorkshire and Lancashire 2-4-2Ts would have given them a run for their money!

These 'Lanky' tanks once worked over half of all the L & Y's passenger traffic. Built at Horwich between 1889-1909, early models weighed-in at 59.2 tons, later models went up to 66 tons.

Distinguished by a sort of 'whinnying' sound when

It's a hazy sort of day in Leeds city centre as No.42113, a Class MT 2-6-4, pulls away from the now long gone Central Station with a local passenger for Bradford. August 2, 1952. *Neg.No.27/C652*

running at passenger speeds, this was the only 2-4-2T type in England to work express trains. Most of the class were fitted with a special type of water pick-up gear to allow them to 'top-up' their tanks when running in either direction. A total of 123 passed into BR hands and the original engine — No.1008 — was restored for preservation at York.

Among the more unusual tanks in Britain was the 'Met' type of the Metropolitan which was designed to reduce smoke, steam and general 'clag' generated by dense traffic on the underground sections of the Metropolitan District Railway, in the years before electrification in 1903-07. They were fitted with a simple type of condensing gear which also helped conserve water.

As for the best-loved tanks — they were probably the Brighton 'Terriers' of the London, Brighton & South Coast Railway. Despite their small size, these 0-6-0T jobs (built 1872 to 1880) did sterling work on the South and East London lines. It was estimated that each one made 172 station stops each working day.

Of course, not all tank engines were on the small side, even if they did carry their water supplies in saddle, well or pannier tanks. Some German, Bavarian, Austrian and Polish tank engines came in very large sizes and carried almost everything from smoke deflectors to kitchen sinks with them; especially in terms of outside plumbing.

Chariot racing was never like this — a Leeds-Ilkley train is overtaken by a York-Bradford service headed by former LMS 2-6-2 No.40169 on June 24, 1952. *Neg.No.1/C642*

It's March, 1958 and 2-6-2 No.40148 clanks into Arthington with a stopping train. Introduced in 1935, the 3P Class weighed 72 tons 10cwt; had a pressure of 200lbs; 5ft 3ins driving wheels and a tractive effort of 21,485lbs. This particular engine was rebuilt and fitted with a larger boiler in 1941. *Neg.No.BIW 36*

Also headed for Arthington: No.80117 cruises down the grade from Bramhope Tunnel as shadows start to lengthen across the face of Otley Chevin on a lovely summer's evening in 1957. *Neg.No BIW 44*

Enough to bring tears to the eyes of older 'Leeds Loiners' who lived south of the River Aire, this picture reeks with the railway atmosphere which stemmed from the 'cat's cradle' of lines just west of the city centre. Class C12 4-4-2 67372 is pictured on a three-coach local train with the interesting backdrop of the now long-vanished Holbeck (High Level) Station on November 22, 1951. *Neg.No.6/C605*

British Railways had been nationalised for almost four months when this Class 3 2-6-2T posed for the cameraman on March 18, 1948, but the locomotive still bore its LMS title and number. Later it became BR No.40195. *Neg.No.4/258C*

November 22, 1951, and 2-6-2- No.41255 was passing through Holbeck (High Level), the low winter sun almost bringing a 'Thomas' touch to the smoke box door. *Neg.No.4/C605*

Putting A Name To It

TIME was when people used to dress up in something decent when they were going on a journey. It was all part of the 'romance of travel', especially if it was to be by sea (which likely involved a 'boat train') and later by air. The name of the game lay in being able to tell friends and acquaintances after the event, the name of the conveyance…'Queen Mary', 'Empress of Canada', 'Pan American China Clipper', BOAC 'Canopus' etc.

The great trains, too, had great names — 'The Golden Arrow', 'The Empire Builder', 'The Broadway Limited', 'Orange Blossom Special', 'The Flying Scotsman' and 'The Indian Pacific' among them. Sadly, in all forms of travel, many of those great names have gone, especially for the trains, and although some remain, and others have been added, they hardly have the charisma of the all-time-greats.

Perhaps it all started to slide with the on-rush of package tours; after all, there is little romantic about a seat-pitch between aircraft seats which allows you to read the newspaper of the chap in front; or the fact that it is possible on some airlines to travel from one side of the world to the other in jeans and trainers — even in Business Class; and cruise ships with near-24-hour programmes of activity are a form of maritime torture that many thought went out with clipper ships.

Thankfully, there are signs world-wide that a new strata of passenger is emerging — and not necessarily having to be rich — who demands something better than 'sardine can travel and everything to a price'. Perhaps passenger power will demand something akin to trains of yore… some of which are pictured here.

The 'Yorkshire Pullman' at Highfield on the way out of Leeds, A1 No.60118 'Archibald Sturrock', in charge. *Neg.No.3/744S*

Different day, different train — but the same engine. 'Archibald Sturrock' takes 'The Queen of Scots' Pullman, towards central Leeds on August 1, 1952. Note the driver with cap-back-to-front, as with early motorcyclists, and certainly when baseball caps were no better known in Leeds than were Hershey chocolate bars. *Neg.No.4/C651*

'The Flying Scotsman' train was as famous around the world as the 'Flying Scotsman' locomotive; the trouble was most people didn't know the difference between one and t'other; just as many of today's younger radio and television journalists refer to locomotives as 'trains' and have picked up the American habit of referring to railway stations as 'train stations' — something which irritates long-time railway employees. After all, what other kind of station was there that mattered much? The engine here, incidentally, is No.60023, 'Golden Eagle', one of the Class A4s which did not enjoy the convenience of a corridor through the tender for the benefit of crews. *Neg.N/A*

One of the finest products of Yorkshire craftsmen, Doncaster-built LNER Pacific 'The Tetrarch' heads a train specially-favoured by Yorkshire business people — 'The Yorkshire Pullman'. Pictured at Hadley Wood Tunnel in 1935, the locomotive was already ten years old, but only a quarter of the way through its life — proof of quality! *Neg.No.RAIL 14*

Not quite what it looks — A4 No.60019 'Bittern' was the last of its class running regularly on BR until only a short time before this picture was taken in November, 1966. Starting out from Leeds for Edinburgh, the engine carried the nameplate of 'The Waverley' named train but this was, in fact, an enthusiasts' special as 'Bittern' began its new life as a preserved locomotive. *Neg.No.RAIL 16*

A1 No.60153 'Flamboyant' makes easy work of hauling the Harrogate portion of 'The Yorkshire Pullman' through Arthington and up the gradient towards Bramhope Tunnel in March, 1958. *Neg.No.BIW16*

Taken at almost the same spot as the last print, but two months later when the trees were in full leaf, A3 No.60081 'Shotover' was hauling 'The Queen of Scots' Pullman on the Glasgow-Edinburgh-Harrogate-Leeds-London route. *Neg.No.BIW 88*

Looking forever LMS, although it has 'British Railways' on its tender, this engine confirmed the statement by retaining its London Midland & Scottish number (with an 'M' prefix added by BR on the smoke box door plate). Above that was another proud name - 'The South Yorkshireman'. Other LMS links are emphasised by the warehouse in the background bearing a sign: 'Lancashire & Yorkshire Railway Goods Depot'. *Neg.No.RAIL 15*

Leeds Town Hall's dome and a clutch of factory chimneys reach for the sky as the 'no messing about' sharp lines of A1 No.60118 'Archibald Sturrock' cause no offence to the eye as they meet the gracious string of coaches which made up the 'Yorkshire Pullman'. The departure station was Leeds Central: August 2, 1952. *Neg.No.26/C652*

It used to be possible to see both the north and southbound 'The Thames-Clyde Express' standing alongside each other at Leeds City Station. Here's the proof: on October 8, 1951, 'Jubilee' Class No.45651 'Shovell', heading the train for London St Pancras, is alongside the service to Glasgow. *Neg.No.6/C594*

With 'Shovell' away (no pun intended), the train on the left, drawn by 'Royal Scot' Class 6P 'Seaforth Highlander' pulled out with the northbound train. And you can bet it made the day for the lone spotter, dressed in the 'sensible' clothes of the period. *Neg.No.8/C594*

There were occasions when 'The Thames-Clyde Express' had something unusual in the lead — as with this 'Black Five' No.44755; one of several of its class fitted with Caprotti valve gear, and nicknamed 'elbows' or 'bow legs' by some of the footplate crews. *Neg.No.1/C594*

A Forceful Reminder Taught Me Better

E. Jobling

ON a visit to Worsboro Fair, we had to cross the old railway goods line that ran up to Penistone and Manchester.

The memories came flooding back; it was hard to believe the amount of traffic that went up there from Wath and beyond; a train every 20 to 30 minutes, and mostly they were heavy coal trains.

We used to be positioned just higher up the line at Wentworth, on the banking engines. About six were stationed there, including the huge 'Garratt', the others were mainly wartime 'Austerity' engines.

It was our job to shove the goods trains up to Silkstone, Penistone, or Dunford, depending on the weight; this being one of the steepest inclines in Yorkshire.

We took it in turns, sometimes using two banking engines, otherwise just the one. The line passed through some beautiful countryside, right up on the moors.

I remember a particular day in the 1940s. I was only about 17 at the time. After we had banked a goods train up to the top, it was the fireman's job to go out and alter the lamps before making the return journey; making sure that the tail lamp showed red. It was a task I nearly always forgot to do, and the driver would have to remind me: but not after this particular night.

We had reached the top and I must have been sitting there day dreaming again when… WHACK!

I wondered whatever had happened, and then realised that my driver had given me a 'back-hander' across the face. He looked at me and just said two words: "THE LAMPS."

I got down quick off the footplate, promising myself I would give him one back when I was a bit older. At that time the driver concerned was 6ft tall and weighed about 15 stones. I was a nine stone matchstick.

A few weeks later, I was partnered again with that same driver. At the end of an incident-free shift he turned and gave me a grin and said: "Tha nivver forgot t'leets (lamps) once."

I grinned back at him, realising he had cured me of a bad habit. And from then on we became good friends.

Mr Jobling lives at Smithies, Barnsley.

For such a well-regarded train, the headboard of 'The White Rose' might have been fixed in a more easily visible position. This placing just above the buffer beam might have suited the clean slope of an A4 streamliner, but looked like an afterthought on A3 'Pacific' 60046 'Diamond Jubilee' on the way out of Leeds for London. *Neg.No.2/543R*

'The Northumbrian', Newcastle-London express, at speed near Doncaster on June 26, 1952, behind A3 No.60112 'St Simon' which featured on the cover of Volume Two of the original set of *Yorkshire Steam* handbooks. *Neg.No.9/C642*

Double Vision of Power in Action

A POWERFUL steam locomotive at full stretch, particularly on a long passenger train, was a sight to behold and thrilled small boys and older enthusiasts alike; but it was only half as good as a 'double-header'.

When a second engine had to be employed to help move a particularly long or heavy train, then you could see power, rather than poetry in motion.

Jealous of their lists of engines seen, young spotters rarely took the precaution of asking a pal to get the front engine's number whilst they took note of the back one. That would have denoted a certain lack of skill. And there was always the danger that young rail fans would be so busy gawping at the exhilarating sight of two big 'uns pounding along, they might even forget to note either number!

Without doubt — as can be seen by the examples printed here — double-headers did look important and taking them from A to B required an extra touch of skill and responsibility on the part of the two footplate crews.

Asked if he had to be a bit of a mind reader to know what the driver of the other engine was about to do, an old driver on the second (train) engine commented: "No, but it helps if it's a chap you know well."

Across the Atlantic, where fearsome gradients caused problems both going up and down sections of line in the Alleghenies coal country, on Sherman Hill, Wyoming and over Donner Pass in the Far West, trains often had to be split and moved in two sections with one engine pulling and another — perhaps two– pushing (see the Transatlantic Trains section).

This led to heart-stopping moments — and a good deal of ear trouble — for the caboose occupants on freight trains: not only was the noise of the pusher engine's exhaust 'stack' immediately behind them utterly deafening, there was always the danger, in the days of early wooden cabooses, that the locomotive would shove its way through the whole contraption — and sometimes did — if the driver was careless with the throttle.

If that sounds like power at its most fearsome, consider the sophisticated power available in America and Canada today on such gradients where it is not unusual, with trains well over a mile in length and weighing 10,000 tons

STEAM TALES

My Black Day In The Tunnel

B.Barker

I SERVED my apprenticeship as a joiner in the Engineer's Department at Low Moor, Bradford, and had a good deal of experience working on bridges and in tunnels. This story relates to the latter.

Such work required the closing of one line, so advance notice had to be given in order that the details of traffic restrictions were known to all departments likely to be affected. When they had all given their clearance, arrangements would be made for the use of an engine, driver and guard, and the necessary staff.

Water was penetrating into this particular tunnel, so the idea was to fix boards to the roof and divert the flow to the sides. My job was to drill the roof, put in wooden plugs and fix the boards.

We had a specially-made truck which had to be pushed by hand through the tunnel as the use of an engine at such close quarters would have near blinded us with smoke, let alone choke us! Even so drilling upwards with sooty water pouring down was decidedly unpleasant!

On completion of the work, the truck was pushed out of the tunnel where I became the laughing stock of all the men on the job – I looked as if I had been black-leaded and polished. Most amused of all was my father who was in charge of this particular job.

The truck we used was known as the 'bull truck' because it had been specially adapted for this purpose and even set up to measure the contours of tunnels for out-of-gauge loads.

Mr Barker, aged 77, lives at Kitson Hill Road, Mirfield.

or more, to have seven diesels up front, with two more cut into the middle of the train and two or three more pushing at the back; the last five of these engines being under radio control from the cab of the leading engine!

Such 'lash-ups' are not simply to add more 'heave' to get the train up a gradient in one section; the power of their accumulated dynamic braking is also required to keep it under control when coming down.

The double-headers pictured here never had quite the same problem…

A Leeds to Liverpool train moving away from City Station with 'Jubilee' Class 45709 'Implacable' and unrebuilt 'Royal Scot' 46137 'The Prince of Wales's Volunteers (South Lancashire) in charge on December 12, 1952. *Neg.No.7/C674*

Harrogate was long-famous as a 'queen of watering places' but the only 'watering place' in the minds of the two crews of these begrimed goods engines would no doubt be one selling somewhat stronger drink as they clanked steadily into town with a heavy train on November 29, 1951. In the lead is Class J39 0-6-0 64855 with 'Austerity' Class WD 2-8-0 90426 providing substantial assistance. In these days of telephones which can fit in the palm of your hand, the 11-crossbar telephone pole on the left serves as a reminder of how far the communications industry has advanced. *Neg.No.2/C608*

Before the closure of the Harrogate-Northallerton line, it was normal for some expresses to be routed via Ripon instead of York. Here an 11-coach train doubleheaded by D49 62753 'The Belvoir' and B1 61069 draws into Harrogate. November 29, 1951. *Neg.No.9/C608*

Something of a mixed bag of rolling stock trails this puffing pair: an unrebuilt version of the 'Royal Scot' Class, No.46137 'The Prince of Wales's Volunteers (South Lancashire)' is the train engine being assisted from the front by 'Jubilee' Class 45631 'Tanganyika' on a Newcastle to Liverpool express making good going out of Leeds. in January, 1953. *Neg.No.1/744S*

It's high summer and the firemen, with everything running in good order, take a breather as these two engines head a Leeds-Carlisle train in July, 1959. 'Black Five' 44675 is aiding an unidentified 'Jubilee'. *Neg.No.BIW 3*

A 'Hunt' Class and an A3 double-up to give extra power for a Liverpool-bound express. Class D49 62762 'The Fernie' — of a class once regularly seen on the Leeds-Harrogate line — pilots an unidentified 'Pacific' back in 1959. The first three coaches are in early BR 'blood and custard' livery, most of the others sport the later maroon finish. *Neg.No.BIW 80*

Pictured from the 'back end' with the photographer probably muttering about a lamp standard and chimney top which have spoiled so many good railway pictures, 'Royal Scot' Class 46137 makes another appearance, this time at Leeds City with 'Jubilee' 45709 'Implacable' ready to do its stuff up front on the 2.58pm to Liverpool. December 12, 1952. *Neg.No.5/C674*

Enjoying a whiff of Wharfedale fresh air, footplate men on a Liverpool-bound train face the setting sun before plunging into the blackness of Bramhope tunnel between Harrogate and Leeds. With 13 coaches on the train they will welcome its re-emergence at Cookridge. In front is D49 'The Fernie', seen giving assistance once again. The 'Pacific' acting as train engine cannot be identified from this angle. *Neg.No.BIW 80*

Humble Goods Engines

IT HAS often been said that what happens in the USA today will happen in Britain in 10 years' time. But the uncertainties of present day life mean that even such a well-worn (and sometimes proven) phrase could not be relied upon to pre-judge a situation, and certainly not to put money on it.

With the emergence of mega railroads in the USA over the past two decades, a process still going on, no one could have guessed that humble 'short lines' operating small 'way freights' calling at factories and depots along 100 miles or so of track would make a comeback; or new ones emerge, especially outfits which would literally become international players almost overnight (eg the Wisconsin Central).

Time was when goods of every kind were trundled around Britain on humble goods trains.

They were as much a part of rural Britain as village churches and pubs, and the clanking of their loose-coupled wagons, the ringing of colliding buffers and 'peeps' of

whistles in the night can still be remembered by old men who had grown up with them when Model T Ford flatbed wagons were still in their infancy.

The engines which hauled such trains were often nondescript, rarely spotless, straightforward in looks and quite simple in terms of working. As with other modest items and people in life, they did the job without much fuss and often over a lifetime. Many of them certainly paid their way many times over and had quite remarkable long service records.

Some were plain, others were ugly, some were so simple they looked like little more than boilers on wheels (the LMS Class 7F, ex-Lancashire & Yorkshire was among them). LMS Class 2F 0-6-0s were well-travelled, as were the GWR's '2800' Class 2-8-0s and Class 2251 0-6-0s. In the North-Eastern area, the Q6 Class 0-8-0s and Gresley's J39 0-6-0s could be seen hauling anything and everything.

Pictured here are samples of the breed…

There's a fair amount of muck among the coal in the tender of Class J6 0-6-0 No.64208 at Holbeck, Leeds. Which might account for the not exactly happy look on the face of the fireman. Above him rises some of the then latest signal technology in the shape of bits of wire, linking chains, pulley wheels, rocker brackets, etc. But all nicely topped-out. November 22, 1951. *Neg.No.9/C605*

A former Midland Railway 0-6-0 (BR No.58212) at Stourton, Leeds, on July 31, 1952. This easily-identified, adaptable class combines the old outline of an outside-frame tender and veteran front-end with a cab roof ventilator which admirers of Santa Fe and Union Pacific EMD-made diesels might easily confuse with their roof-top air-conditioning equipment — in another setting. As it was, the BR crew could get all the air-conditioning they needed, especially when running in reverse. *Neg.No.5/C649*

There were none of the horrors of the M62 and M1 around, and the 'Information Superhighway' had never been thought of when Class J39 No.64934 was 'out the road' with a mixed goods, puffing its way through leafy glades on the approach to Bramhope Tunnel (length 2 miles 241 yards), running on track whose ballast had been kept neatly in line. August, 1958. *Neg.No.BIW 28*

An easy load for former LMS 2P 4-4-0 No.40685, trundling a tank wagon and brake van along at Stainforth, near Settle, in June, 1958. *Neg.No.BIW 15*

Mucky? — yes. Mundane? well… not quite: everyday scenes such as this at Wortley South, Leeds, summed-up the short to medium-haul mixed freight business which made up much of the goods traffic before the juggernauts burst upon a less-hurried world. Bits of this, bits of that, a wagon load of t'other and a no-nonsense Class 01/4, numbered 63584 moves sturdily by, watched by a fussy J50 tank engine. *Neg.No.D711/5*

Goole-based LMS Class 2F 2-6-0 No.6405. This useful class was one of several types which continued to appear for from the workshops some time after nationalisation. March 23, 1948. *Neg.No.3/258C*

You would not find many track sections like this on the average Hornby layout: No.43130 with various instructions chalked on its buffers, clanks past the north end of York Station with a short goods train made up of plank-sided wagons and mainly steel vans. The former have no doubt gone to the great goods yard in the sky; the latter might well have fetched up in some farm yard, allotment or hen-pen, their once lingering aromas of fish, chemicals, benzine or what-have-you long wafted away. The massive diamond cross-over, a tribute to British track-construction expertise, is also long gone. December 29, 1952. *Neg.No.4/C677*

Proud Names Graced Gresley Pacifics

THE NAME of Sir Nigel Gresley is synonymous with that of the 'Pacific' type of steam locomotive. There were bigger and sleeker types, but of all the Pacifics built for the LNER the A3 Class was arguably the most adaptable.

The original Gresley Pacifics were introduced in 1922. These engines had 6ft 8in diameter driving wheels, weighed 92 tons 9cwt, and had tenders weighing 56 tons 6cwt.

The A3 class, represented here by 'Woolwinder', 'Tagalie' and 'Sir Hugo' was introduced in 1927 as a development of the GNR A1 Class. Some A3s were rebuilds of that model. A few retained their Great Northern-type tenders fitted with coal rails (as with 'Woolwinder' and 'Sir Hugo') others had the more modern LNER type (as with 'Manna').

Although they did not exude the glamour of the 'designer engine' A1s or the sophistication of the streamlined A4s, they had something going for them, for one of their class bore the LNER number 4472 and was called 'Flying Scotsman'. She was, and probably still is, the most famous engine in the world (see Flying Scotsman section).

Others in the class might have been lesser stars but among them were locos whose names were revered by young enthusiasts: 'Captain Cuttle', 'Royal Lancer', 'Knight of the Thistle', 'Cameronian', 'Prince of Wales', 'Dick Turpin' and 'Spion Kop'. Resounding names indeed, and a far cry from some of the commercially-inspired 'wet' names that do little for some latter-day diesel and electric locomotives.

Yorkshire-built and Yorkshire-based — A3 No.60055, with an appropriate name in a county famed for its woollen products: 'Woolwinder'. It was on its way from Copley Hill shed to Leeds Central Station to head the 3.20pm express to London when this picture was taken on August 1, 1952.
Neg.No.10/C651

On stand-by at Doncaster Station, A3 No.60064 'Tagalie' with the newer-style high-sided tender but the older type steam dome which not did not have the 'streamlined' fairing. March 27, 1952. *Neg.No.22/C625*

The tail-end of 'Sir Hugo' (which has the 'streamlined' fairing on its steam dome), merges with a mixture of coaches, pillars, roof girders and brac- ing, light and shadow in the old Leeds City Station. (At the time of writing, the station buildings which replaced most of it are themselves due for a £25 million refurbishment as a part of Railtrack's investment on infrastructure over the next ten years). December 12, 1952. *Neg.No.4/C674*

Getting All Steamed Up

A SCENE in a Australian railway video depicts the commentator bending down outside Sydney Central Station and picking-up a piece of coal. "This," he says, almost reverently, "is what used to make it all go."

Well, that plus the water which was turned into steam, plus quite a few other odds and ends. But it is the steam we are looking at in this section.

When environment was a word lots of people had to look up in a dictionary, trains like these plied their way twixt one place and another without a murmur of complaint.

Unless, of course, it was Aunty Annie who caught a minute cinder in her eye when she lowered the compartment window as the train entered Ripon, or cousin Maude who got a couple of spots on her blouse between Malton and York.

But for small boys and grandads all this smoke and the associated aromas were a joy: the real thing as one of the world's top advertising slogans was later to proclaim in another context. The sheer joy that came from a whiff of all that smoke and hot oil plus the muggy sort of warmth that ebbed and flowed from the groaning floor level steam heaters in winter was the only kind of fix enthusiasts needed to send them into ecstasy in those days.

The sight of such emissions on a regular basis these days would have some members of the population going near orbital. It is just as well they do not patronise those steam excursions, especially in the US where the fans want nothing better than to take pictures of locomotives as they used to be, running full out and working hard. So the engine driver stops to drop off all those clutching cameras, video and sound equipment. Then he backs up his train for a couple of miles, wets his finger and holds it up to judge the wind direction, then opens the throttle (regulator in UK terms) and the old oil burner he's driving responds with gusto and throws out a black smoke screen fit to hide a fleet of battleships.

Whoooeee — that's what you call getting 'all steamed-up'.

The uninitiated might well be persuaded that J39/1 No.64835 was leaking badly as the 0-6-0 drew a train of mixed wagons and vans through Neville Hill, Leeds on November 27, 1951. *Neg.No.15/C607*

A rather more distinguished front end is almost enveloped in steam as 60029 'Woodcock' waits to move off from Copley Hill for an express run that will see steam coming out 'topsides' at a much more rapid rate than this. August 1, 1952. *Neg.No.16/C651*

'Sir Vincent Raven' was well steamed up with safety valves streaming as she awaited the call of duty at Neville Hill Depot on November 27, 1951. (Also see 'On Shed' section of this book). *Neg.No.1/C607*

Forgotten Church Fenton Connection…

Roy Pearson

YEARS ago, when you asked young lads what they wanted to be when they grew up, most would reply: "An engine driver." In my case it was never to be, but for many years I achieved the next best thing: I was a railway fireman.

I well remember one particular shift which consisted of four hours shunting carriages in and out of Leeds City Station, making up trains for various destinations; then backing on to our own train – the 6.40pm Church Fenton Roundabout.

It got its name because it went round in a loop, leaving Leeds via Garforth and returning via Collingham and Scholes. It called at every station, dropping off home-going workers on the way out and then people going into town for a night out on the way back.

On this occasion, because the water for the engine was depleted after shunting, it was necessary to top-up the tender tank at the platform water tower.

As we backed on to the waiting coaches of the Church Fenton train, we were ideally-placed for the tower. I swung the water bag across, climbed to the top of the tender to ensure the water went into the right place, my driver turned the valve and inside a few minutes she was filled up.

Climbing back into the engine cab, I began to attend to the firebox. It was already primed to the front, but needed turning over and slightly 'salt and peppering' – three or four shovels of coal sprinkled around the box. This done, I settled down on my seat and looked back along the platform for the 'off' signal from the guard; having already noted that the old semaphore-type signals were at green.

First came the whistle, then the green flag. "Right away," I said to my driver. He re-sponded by giving the usual pull on the regulator… but never before had we had such a response.

The engine took off as if jet-propelled – to the amazement of my driver, the signalman in his box and, most of all, myself. It was a fair distance before we could bring her to a halt.

The cause of this amazing start was simple: I had forgotten to couple the engine to the train.

To say the signalman was annoyed (we were causing an amount of chaos) would be an understatement. He used words I had never previously heard to tell us that he had never seen such a fiasco; did not believe it could happen and hoped it never would happen again. He then switched the points and gave us permission to return the train.

His comments, and the ribald remarks and assorted advice from the passengers leaning out of all the windows rang in my ears for days afterwards. Yes, it really was my most embarrassing moment – and one I was never allowed to forget.

Mr Pearson lives in Brignall Croft, Leeds.

Looking as if it was leaking from every joint, 2-6-0 No.43098 was one of a 'Jack of all trades' class used on local passenger and freight work. The 4MT Class engine was at Leeds City on December 12, 1952. *Neg.No.2/C674*

There wasn't much left of the view of Copley Hill shed, Leeds, as Class V2 2-6-2 No.60869 headed out of Leeds, its progress marked by a large pall of smoke and steam. *Neg.No.D711/7.*

One small chimney making more smoke than ten large ones behind it — 'Black Five' No.44854 in early BR days, with a rake of former LMS coaches in 'blood and custard' paint. *Neg.No.2/548R*

From the front page of the Spring 1997, edition of *Portraits of Steam*, No.62738 'The Zetland' of the popular-in-Yorkshire 'Hunt' Class takes to the Otley curve off the Harrogate-Leeds main line at Arthington North in February, 1958. *Neg.No.BIW/32*

Class B1 4-6-0 No.61062 envelopes itself and passengers on the platform in steam on arrival at Harrogate Station on November 29, 1951. *Neg.No.5/C608*

Leeds City Station

IT'S EARLY evening on April 23, 1962, wind out of the south-west and Peter Rose, who has taken many fine pictures for use in the *Portraits of Steam* series of tabloids, was there to take this panoramic view of one of Britain's best known city stations.

The picture is split, almost centrally, with the old Wellington Station (Leeds City North) on the left, and Leeds New Station, or Leeds City South, on the right. On the extreme left is the Post Office clock tower in City Square followed by (left to right), the old signal box which retained its original name of Leeds Wellington. The tall building beyond the box was the BR Divisional Office in Aire Street (many ex-Servicemen across the country might well recall its use as an RTO's office in World War Two). Then comes the back of the Queen's Hotel, with the 1938 North Concourse running clean across the line of sight to the spire of Trinity Church, where starts the roof

line of the old train sheds of Leeds New Station or Leeds City South.

The right-hand half of the picture is dominated by Leeds City West signal box, replaced by a new signalling centre when the new Leeds Station was built following the closure of Leeds Central in 1967. All the area behind the West Box and to the right of the train sheds has been re-developed, as has that on the extreme left of the picture; today the whole skyline, clean across the picture, has a different look.

This is not the first city centre station in Leeds. That honour went to the Wellington Station of the Leeds & Bradford Railway (incorporated July 4, 1844), which was tucked away at the east end of Wellington Street, near the site of the original Queen's Hotel. In fact, much of the station was located where a sparkling new complex of buildings will take ever-changing Leeds into the 21st century.

Wellington Station was a somewhat complicated structure, with its large train sheds spanning the River Aire and a labyrinth of underground passages.

'Railway Mania' — an era of rapid expansion of railways — was about to burst upon Britain and soon several lines were vying to get passenger and goods facilities as near as possible to the centre of Leeds. All manner of plans were drawn up, the most ambitious being that of John Hawkshaw for a 900ft long, 400ft wide structure running from Monk Bridge, south of the city centre, to Infirmary Street, off City square, at a then astronomical cost of £258,000, Had it gone ahead, the face of Leeds centre today would be totally different.

However, an unholy row broke out between the competing railway companies and a series of political skirmishes followed. In the event, these led to a concentration of ideas for the already existing Central Station (see elsewhere in this book), which was not 'central' in a physical or commercial sense, and the subsequent transfer of trains to Wellington Station, nearer the city centre, soon found the latter establishment becoming clogged as the Midland, London & North Western, North Eastern and Lancashire & Yorkshire Railways sought to gain terminus near the centre.

Even today, a line drawn from east to west across central Leeds reveals that only one railway — the Leeds to Harrogate line inaugurated by the Leeds & Thirsk Railway, actually penetrates that drawn line. Yet south of it in the old days railways soared, swooped, ducked and dived and went over and under each other at various levels in order to feed the demands of the rapidly-growing city and its industries, particularly those south of the Aire.

At times the situation was near-chaotic, with (some would say 'as ever') the passengers suffering most. The situation revealed a lack of central control or direction which, more recently, has again underlined the lack of a co-ordinated transport policy in Britain.

The congestion at Wellington Station led to demands for better services east of Leeds and the North Eastern agreed on the need for a line to be carried on a viaduct from near Wellington to Marsh Lane, which had been the terminus of the Leeds & Selby Railway since 1834. Along with its viaduct proposal, the North Eastern also agreed to build a station to be known as Leeds New Station, along with the London & North Western company, to the south of Wellington Station …and the eventual 'City Station' was on its way.

But it was not until 1938 that moves were made to

physically connect the Wellington and New Station structures, which were often referred to thereafter as City North and City South. That year a splendid light and airy concourse, ahead of its time in Britain and likened to American practice with a 'gate' system of entry to platforms, was built by the LMS Railway behind the Queen's Hotel and generally referred to as the North Concourse. But the LMS and LNER still held out against fully combining the two stations and it was not until after nation-

alisation that a 'one station' scheme, costing £4.5 million, was begun in 1959. Capital expenditure cuts 'stopped the job' in 1961 and there were further cuts when work restarted in 1963. And so Leeds City Station came into being.

Leeds City North became a parcels depot and the splendid concourse behind the Queen's Hotel was tragically allowed to fall from grace when it was put to use as a car park until a decision could be made on its future.

The Midland Railway had a large sign facing City Square to mark its Wellington Station, Leeds, in this 1921 view. But some predecessor of today's 'put adverts on anything, whether it moves or not', brigade, had persuaded the Midland to let him put an even bigger sign for Archibald Ramsden's pianos on the gable end of the station entrance. The soot-blackened outline of the original Queen's Hotel rears on the left. One wonders why an outfit as canny with its brass as was the Midland would have erected such a defensive array of formidable columns and gates to guard its station? *Neg.N/A*

Eastenders — This picture of Class D20 No.62397 running through Marsh Lane, Leeds, in the Spring 1995, edition of *Portraits of Steam* raised consid-erable interest, if only because the photograph had been taken 50 years after the engine went into service in 1899. Here's a picture of a sister engine, No.62341, also arriving at Leeds City having just passed through the east end of the city on its way from Selby. *Neg.N/A*

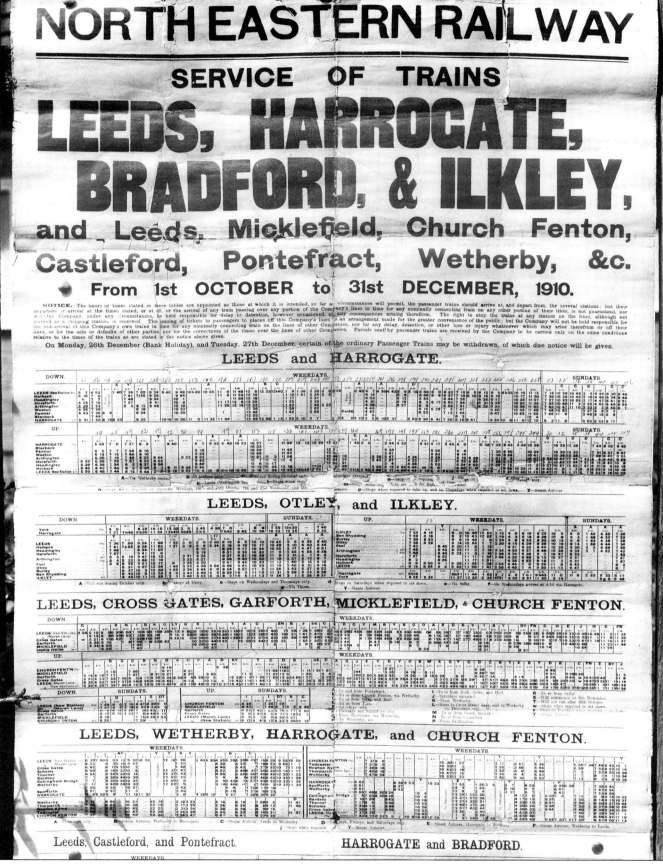

The accent is surely on the word 'Service' in this North-Eastern Railway poster covering October to December, 1910. 'Rat run' specialists; those subject to 'Road Rage'; victims of 'White Knuckle Driving' or 'Wake me up when the lights change' syndrome and general rush-hour lunacy will no doubt note with interest that nearly 90 years ago it was possible to catch a train from Harrogate and be in Leeds city centre in 40 minutes There were trains from Horsforth that took less than 20 minutes including two stops; folks from Ilkley could also make it with or bah't 'at, in 40; and if you were lucky enough to be domiciled at Pool in Wharfedale, you could leave your idyllic home surroundings, pluck a rose from the garden for your lapel, catch the train, and de-train in Leeds in 32 minutes with the dew still on your bloom! Just a small point: in small print the North Eastern had a disclaimer on the poster advising that the company 'could not guarantee departure or arrival at the time stated, or at all'. But you can bet there were more trains on time than there were needing to be covered by the disclaimer. *Neg.No.BIW/1A*

Smoke from three-cylinder 'Compound' No.41080 mingles with the chimney pots of central Leeds at City Station. These good-looking, comparatively small 4-4-0s were capable of a remarkable turn of speed for their size. October 8, 1951. *Neg.No.2/C594*

A Newcastle-Liverpool train slows down for its Leeds stop under the command of A3 No.60083 'Sir Hugo' on December 12, 1952. *Neg.No.3/C674*

'Jubilee' Class No.45705 'Seahorse' near-obliterates the view from Leeds City West Box with a powerful screen of smoke and steam as it gets into its stride.
Neg.No.3/C677

Pictured from the Canal Basin in much more recent times, the long brick viaduct which the North Eastern Railway agreed to build from near the then Wellington Station to Marsh Lane in the east of the city, runs across the centre of this picture. The Leeds New Station (see main picture at the start of this section) was at approximately the point where the diesel locomotive is standing on the viaduct. Outside of the viaduct, and Canal Basin stonework, all the structures in this picture have appeared in the last 30 years or so.
Neg.No.1811942/3

Marsh Lane Cutting

SURPRISINGLY for a big city that lay at the gateway to the crowded mill areas of the Heavy Woollen District to the south and west, and the equally-packed mills of Bradford; the first railway into Leeds came not from the land of 'dark satanic mills', but from a market town to the east — via a dark satanic tunnel (see 'Tunnels Come, Tunnels Go' section), and a deep, steeply-graded cutting.

Apart from some deep sandstone cuttings (some of which were originally tunnels), there was little in England to beat Marsh Lane, Leeds, in terms of a great gash in the ground. Deep cuttings allowed trains of the Liverpool & Manchester Railway (1830) to climb from the west to ground that would allow a more level approach to Manch-

ester. But children of the 1990s are unlikely ever to set eyes upon these older urban cuttings memorable for their smells, slipping wheels, clanking catch-points and soot-grimed walls. Once Marsh Lane Cutting had been opened up to accommodate four tracks (the obnoxious tunnel had been 'daylighted' as the Americans would have put it, in the 1890s it became a great place for spotting important cross-country expresses, especially those between Lancashire's main cities and the North-East.

It also became a notorious dumping ground (and still is) for rubbish of all types: bedsteads, bicycles and supermarket trolleys.

Class B16/2 No.61475 blasts unburnt coal dust out of her chimney along with steam as she charges through Marsh Lane, site of the original Leeds & Selby terminus, on November 15, 1951, heading for 'the cutting'. *Neg.No.9/C603*

Here's the same engine, a couple of weeks later, putting on another spirited performance as she climbs toward the top end of the cutting. *Neg.No.3/C604*

Global warming? Smog? Blame it on car exhausts and fossil fuels? Forty-five years ago, before we had hardly heard of such expressions, Class 8F 2-8-0 No.48673 was making its own (modest at that stage contribution) to the smog gathering toward the upper reaches of Marsh Lane's cutting. Between the tender and the line of tank wagons was a barrier wagon — put there as a precaution. *Neg.No.4/C604*

Another angle on the engine which opened this section — No.61475 — near the top of the steep climb on November 27, 1975. *Neg.No.6/C607*

Having reached the top, let's go down again: A Newcastle-Leeds-Liverpool express powered by A3 No.60092 'Fairway', points its nose towards City Station as it eases into the deeper section of Marsh Lane. November 20, 1951. *Neg.No.2/C604*

Many Unhappy Returns

Colin Smith

BACK in the early 1950s, I was clerk-in-charge of Pontefract Tanshelf Station. It was a rather grandiose title, as I worked mainly on my own. The rest of the 'staff' comprised two porters who worked alternate shifts.

During the Rugby League season the powers-that-be decided to run football specials from Tanshelf to Featherstone for each home match. When the first excursion came I was run off my feet.

About 400 people descended on the station and I had to stamp all the tickets (twice), take the fares and give change through a small aperture that was full of thrusting hands. The train was held up and I was totally frustrated and embarrassed. When I recovered, I sat down to think it out and decided that the only way in future was to stamp all the tickets before the supporters arrived and have numerous piles of change handy.

Came the big day and – you've guessed it – the match was cancelled!

In those days there was a 'Mutilated/Spoilt Ticket' return to send in, which usually had one half ticket attached to it. With mine there were 432 tickets in a large bag.

Next day I had a visit from a bowler-hatted 'heavy' from Leeds who was totally bemused by the whole event which, he said, was unprecedented in the history of British Rail.

The following year I left to go into banking, no doubt to sighs of relief as that was not the only faux pas I made during my railway 'career'.

Mr Smith lives at Whitley, near Goole

Almost enclosed by the massive retaining walls and a bridged section, another A3, (No.60085 'Manna') nears the Leeds starting point of the former Leeds & Selby Railway. November 15, 1951. *Neg.No.1/C603*

And here's where the Leeds & Selby line started in 1834 — Marsh Lane Station in a classic urban setting 45 years ago, with a 'Black Five' easing a goods train out of the cutting. *Neg.No.2/C603*

…and just one more: a long goods train with an interesting variety of vans, clanks out on to the level from the cutting with 2-8-0 No.90640 in charge. These War Department engines were ordered to meet the increased demands of wartime, and later became part of the BR fleet. November 15, 1951. *Neg.No.4/C603*

'Flying Scotsman'

Wherever railway fans meet in the world, there is one name which needs no introduction and here it is. There is little that can be written, or said about 'Flying Scotsman' which has not been written or said thousands times over: if ever there was an engine that suits the phrase: 'Been there, seen it, done it', then this is the one. Yet the very name can still bring a gleam to the eye of great-grandfathers who recall its racing outline well over half-a-century ago on what is now the East Coast Main Line. It crossed the Atlantic to be welcomed by Americans who might well have been confused between 'Flying Scotsman' (the engine) and 'The Flying Scotsman' (the train), having been more likely to have seen the latter in British films. But there was no shame in being confused — the average 'Brit' in the street knew no better — but engine or train, no matter: they both did wonders for the tourist business. And when the locomotive went 'Down Under', ex-pats, and new and old Australians alike gave it welcoming cheers loud enough to be heard almost from Perth, Western Australia, to Perth back in Bonnie Scotland. The compiler, for one, will never forget the sight of three trains, running on parallel tracks, comprising one led by 'Flying Scotsman', the second and third headed by Aussie engines Nos.R707 and R761; and at another venue and even more impressive, the 'Scotsman' double-heading with No.3801, the bullet-nosed beauty that is to Australia what the ex-LNER star is to the UK. *Neg.N/A*

Saved from the scrap heap in the early 1960s by Sheffield businessman Alan Pegler, it wasn't long before the famous engine was being given a thorough overhaul at Darlington Loco Works. *Neg.N/A*

Left: When it came to making her American tour, the 'Scotsman' was fitted-out with a large whistle, mounted on the right-hand side of her smoke box, and a brass bell just ahead and to the right of the smoke box door. These were required by American regulations, as was the knuckle-coupler she was given and a 'cow catcher', or more correctly, pilot. Prior to the trip, additional work was carried out at a Hunslet, Leeds, engineering works where Mr Jimmy Howcroft, then 56, was pictured in the driver's seat checking out her controls. She was loaded aboard the 'Saxonia' at Liverpool on September 19, 1969. *Neg.N/A*

Below: On her eventual return to Britain, on February 13, 1973, after financial problems which have been well-documented, there seemed to be even bigger welcomes for her wherever she went throughout the UK, especially on enthusiasts' specials. *Neg.N/A*

The attention given to preserved engines was not, however, reflected elsewhere in the dying days of BR steam; as is clear in this picture of the 'Flying Scotsman' waiting to take its turn with a 'fan' trip amid what are believed to be the sad remains of Leeds Central Station in its own dying days. *Neg.N/A*

Another day, another trip — enthusiasts young and old were at the platform's end at Wakefield (Kirkgate) in June, 1969, when the 'star' paused briefly on a special train en route to Cleethorpes. *Neg.N/A*

The clean-cut lines that have done so much to give 'Flying Scotsman' such an enduring appeal are self-evident in this shot of her passing through Leeds with another enthusiasts' special in 1971. *Neg.N/A*

Day of pride: built at Doncaster in 1923, the world's most famous steam locomotive hauls engine No.910, built at Gateshead in 1875, in the Stockton & Darlington Railway's 150th anniversary cavalcade in 1975. The older engine pipped the honours on that occasion, having also taken part in the 50th (1875) and 100th (1925) anniversary parades. *Picture: British Railways.*

...but there was a wealth of detail around her — and a vast crowd — when the great lady turned out for her Diamond Jubilee appearance in 1983. Her Class number and place of birth had been added to the buffer beam; and her headboard not only recorded the event but also her connections with the LNER, BR and Steamtown. One thing is clear: had there been a problem, there were enough people around to give her a push start. But then, she's too much of a lady for that, y'ken. *Neg.N/A*

Carrying a headboard for 'The Flying Scotsman' train, the 'Scotsman' engine made a special run from Manchester to York, and a visit to the National Railway Museum, as part of a nostalgic journey with famous rail fan Michael Palin for the television *Great Railways of the World* series. Surprisingly for such a visibly special occasion, some wag, nit or vandal had deliberately mucked-up the number on the buffer beam; or one of the crew had forgotten to buff-off the cleaning fluid! *Neg.N/A*

Black Fives — Spotters' Delight

WHAT was it about LMS 'Black Fives' that made them so popular with steam enthusiasts? They did not have quite the purposeful style of the LNER's better-known engines; or the straightforward lines of the GWR's locos, nor the undeniably 'South of Watford' different look of engines from the Southern Railway's stables — yet their name consistently tripped off enthusiasts' tongues all over Britain.

Perhaps it was because they roamed far and wide, so that their numbers were ticked off wholesale on the pages of spotters' prized 'seen 'em' books. Or was it because the LMS found them to be such good all-round workhorses, which could grace any passenger train when in clean condition, and didn't look out of place and could certainly do their stuff when coupled to a heavy freight train?

Those tapered boilers certainly did something for them in terms of looks.

But anyone who has waited damp-nosed for a Black Five-headed train at Manchester Victoria on a foggy winter's night …or heard the exhaust beat of a Manchester-bound night train climbing towards Marsden …knows that it was the whistle of a Black Five which marked out its individuality.

A cross between 'the buzzers' announcement of shift-change time at a Yorkshire pit, or knocking-off time in a Tyneside shipyard, its deep, commanding note informed everyone within hearing distance so that even on the darkest night, you just knew the train was headed by a Black Five.

Introduced in 1934, a total of 842 were built so that, in due course, it became the largest single class on BR. Some were fitted with Caprotti valve gear, others had roller bearings — which were to become all the rage in the United States — and one (No. 44844) was fitted for oil burning. The engines weighed 72 tons 2cwt, had six-foot driving wheels and a boiler pressure of 225lbs.

No.44853 pounds through Stourton, Leeds, with an express bound for Bristol. London Midland & Scottish Railway enthusiasts claim that the 'Black Fives' were 'the engines which won the war' because of the sterling work they did in many parts of Britain. *Neg.No.1/C695*

Setting out from Leeds City in May, 1948, on a test run over the heavy grades to Carlisle was this then new loco 44754. It was one of the few members of the class to have Caprotti valve gear. *Neg.No.RAIL 13*

Leeds-based No.44828 coasting through Holbeck under all-clear 'pegs down' lower quadrant signals. *Neg.No.8/C605*

'British Railways' it says on the tender. But this 'Black Five', pictured just after nationalisation, still sports the LMS number 5099. The 'M' on the cab side was a temporary mark until re-numbering as BR 45099 was carried out. *Neg.No.5/258C*

A Bradford man who regularly travelled on this line claims that on this Leeds-Bradford early evening commuter train, First and Third class compartments were generally referred to as 'Businessmen' and 'Season Ticket Holders'. Certainly someone decided to make it self-important, for an engine the size of 44658 was hardly necessary to handle such a lightweight consist. Perhaps a BR 'Big Wheel' was on board as it sped through Kirkstall from Tetley's to Webster's country on a pleasant evening in 1952? *Neg.No.5/C642*

Now this was more like it: another 'Black Five', No.44987, runs through Kildwick with an express from Edinburgh to London (St Pancras). Known before World War Two as the 'Thames-Forth Express', the train later had its name changed to 'The Waverley'. *Neg.No.4/479R*

Waiting for its next turn of duty: No.44692 simmers quietly near Holbeck Shed, Leeds, in 1951. *Neg.No.2/C605*

Royal Trains

IN A rapidly-changing world where countless businesses have been pressured into believing that money matters before anything else — even their products it would appear in some cases — it is not surprising that economics have pervaded every corner of society, often bringing with them greed, envy, crime and corruption on a previously unknown scale.

No one has been above this tide of financial fluctuation, so it should have come as no surprise over the past few years that even royal families, world leaders and dignitaries of various religious faiths have been touched by the spume.

Despite that, the railway fraternity — and vast numbers of the public — still admire outstanding examples of period technology that were once a measure of Britain's standing in the world: and not least The Royal Train. It has been the subject of much contention in the past and is once more at the time of writing (May 1997), but for our part here we simply present this section to illustrate yet another aspect of the fascinating world of railways.

Royal trains were not, of course, restricted to Britain or exclusive to the British Royal Family. And in the days of the British Empire, when the Royals were welcomed within its realms across the globe, member countries made the provision of a Royal Train one of their priorities.

In Canada today, the 'Royal Hudson' type of Canadian Pacific locomotive survives in preserved steam as a mark of the respect accorded Royal visitors in the past.

Royal coaches preserved at the National Railway Museum at York have always been one of its main attractions and there are other examples elsewhere.

Back in the 1960s, the British Transport Commission was moved to mount a highly-popular 'Royal Journey' exhibition which highlighted rolling stock and equipment that had been used in connection with Royal journeys over the years. Pictured here is the Caledonian Railway's splendid No.123 engine which was built in 1886 by Neilson & Co, and exhibited at the Edinburgh Exhibition of that year. Its job in relation to Royal trains was to act as 'Royal Train Pilot', as per its headboard; a task which involved it running in advance of the actual Royal Train in order ensure that everything was in order and safe for the passage of the official train.
Photograph: British Transport Commision

In July, 1937, King George V and Queen Mary travelled to Edinburgh on the London Midland & Scottish Royal Train for the Scottish Royal Visit. The rolling stock included these two Royal saloons. *Photograph: Fox Photos Ltd*

This was one of the first photographs to be taken of the interior of the LMS Royal Train before it left Euston. It shows the then Queen's Sleeping Compartment. *Photograph: Fox Photos Ltd*

...and next door was Her Majesty's Day Compartment. *Photograph: Fox Photos Ltd*

Things were somewhat less formal in the lounge of the special train which took the current Queen and HRH The Duke of Edinburgh on part of their tour of New Zealand in 1954. It was decorated in contemporary style in blended pastel shades and its easy chairs, upholstered with foam rubber, were a world away from the furniture in the previous picture. The small dining table could be folded away when not in use into the combination radio and cocktail cabinet-cum-writing desk. The two lamps above the desk were made from red spun aluminium. *Photograph: Sport & General*

Below: And this was the exterior of the New Zealand Railways' Royal Train, which operated on the narrow gauge system. The coaches were painted in crimson lake, with an ivory shade roof and black undergear. The Royal Arms were displayed on each side of the Queen's Coach, in the foreground, which also had an observation platform as the last car on the eight-coach train. *Photograph: Sport & General*

How Jingling George Missed The Train

Graham Kennewell

'JINGLING George', of happy memory, was a driver on the LNER well-known for his ability to prolong a conversation longer than was necessary.

On one occasion he and his fireman booked in at York at 2.00pm – he was rostered on the spare link – and was rostered to go by the 3.00pm passenger train to Selby, there to take another train to its allotted destination.

However, his weakness for a long conversation got the better of him and when he arrived at the station at 3.00pm, the train had left.

George and his mate returned immediately to the York Loco Depot, and, without informing the office, went down to the ash pits where they found a newly-returned locomotive in steam.

They took this loco, No 2355, proceeded to the outgoing signal, informing the signalman: "Light engine to Selby." On getting the all clear off they went and, on arriving at Selby, left the engine at the shed and took over the train for which they were booked. And off they went as originally planned.

Two days later, a mystified supervisor at York was ringing round the region's depots asking if they knew the whereabouts of No 2355? On phoning Selby, he was asked why he was calling.

"Because we've lost an engine," came the surprising reply. Asked the Selby voice: "What number did you say?"

"Number two three five five…"

"Good Lord!" exclaimed the Selby voice, "we've been wondering where that came from. It's been here in steam for the last two days…"

How 'Jingling George' got away with that one, I will never know.

The New Zealand Royal Train's contemporary in the UK at that time was this one: posed for the photographer by British Railways. The former LMS Royal Train, it was built at Wolverton Works on the London Midland Region, and was pictured there. *Photograph: British Railways*

Enginemen Elite

R.Page

THE footplate of a steam locomotive was a hot and dirty environment, yet locomen took a great pride in their appearance.

There were several men at Holbeck who always wore a white collar, and a tie.

One fireman sported a bright dickie bow!

Another top-link fireman could shovel five or six tons of coal on the trip to London, yet on arrival, could step from the footplate looking immaculate.

Many drivers in the top link carried the traditional 'lodging baskets'. These were either metal or wickerwork and being very commodious, they would hold enough food and tea-makings to cover any eventuality, plus the essential driver's notices for the route.

Tea was the universal beverage for engine men, brewed in a white enamelled billy-can which held about one pint. After several hours stewing on the engine boiler's backplate hob, the liquid would take on the consistency, colour and even the taste of brown paint.

For this reason some men preferred tea kept warm in a bottle, the bottle most suited for this purpose being from Johnny Walker whisky or Gordon's gin. They would be obtained from the dining-car stewards and as the bottles were flat-faced they could be wedged between the steam pipes and would not roll off.

V2 Class Had A Good Sense Of Purpose

Although they lacked the smooth lines of Gresley's streamliners, the LNER's V2 Class had a lean, hungry and purposeful look about them. Here at Copley Hill Depot, Leeds, in British Railways livery, is No.60855. Following a good clean, she might have been worthy of the word 'sleek'.

These 2-6-2 engines were introduced by the LNER in 1936. At 6ft 2ins diameter, their driving wheels were smaller than some comparative LMS engines, but North Easterners could manage a fair turn of speed. Each locomotive weighed 93 tons 2cwts and each tender 52 tons. *Neg.No.8/C651*

In The Good Old Days

Les Morton

IN the light of the present water situation, I thought this memory might be of particular interest.

In the days of steam, things were not as hectic as they are today. More time was needed to get up speed and more time was needed to slow down.

Although timetables still had to be complied with, if something caused a holdup there was enough flexibility to catch up and put things right. In current jargon, it was more laid back; you had more elbow room.

So it was with us. We would regularly collect our loco, then do the two-mile trip to pick up the train. On the way we would often see Bert in his Water Board uniform riding his bike on his way to work.

We were looking out for him as usual on this particular morning when we spotted him lying on his side on the ground. His bike was sprawled beside him and his uniform cap had fallen off.

"Bert's been knocked down," shouted the driver and braked the engine suddenly.

We ran across to see what we could do for him: he turned his head towards us with a strained expression. "Don't move," I told him. "I've done first aid and it's better to stay still."

He struggled to get up and I tried to stop him from injuring himself any more.

"Gerroff, yer daft devil," he growled: "I'm only turning this stopcock off."

Mr Marton lives at Windsor Road, Wakefield.

Another angle on a V2: No.60826, also at Copley Hill, looks a mite cleaner than its sister '855', but coal dust washed down the side of her tender hardly helps the image. *Neg.No.7/C651*

This is more like it: No.60921, oiled and polished, heads north out of Doncaster on March 27, 1952. *Neg.No.21/C625*

York Station

UNLIKE their compatriots at 'dead-end' buffer-stop big city stations, where a platform ticket might well guarantee a train spotter 'from the waist up' close-ups of famous locomotives, those enthusiasts who chose York station and its environs as a base for their hobby could see it all.

Famous engines with famous names galloped into this great, curving edifice, paused to gather their strength, then steamed off 'out the line' again, some with "Maybe it's because I'm a Londoner" whistled by their south-bound drivers; others rushing north towards the skirl o' the pipes as Edinburgh beckoned.

Like some of the great railroad centres of America's Midwest, York's mid-country position attracted great trains: big, premium stuff with drivers whose names were known to every spotter schoolboy.

Stand a mile from either end of York station and you could see engineering poetry in motion; trains slowing in one direction; trains gathering speed in another. Strings of coaches, with softly-lit table lamps in the gloaming; white-coated waiters; and in the fire's glow of their cabs, drivers peering ahead, ten-to-one with fob watches in their hands.

Then it was time for the tired spotters to be off for a 'fish an' a penn'orth'. Then home to Henry Hall, or in later years, Joe Loss, or The Goon Show ...with lonesome whistles still echoing among the many spires.

What have we done to lose such innocent, happy days?

Spotters' delight: LNER Pacific No.2552 'Sansovino' passes Waterworks signal box at the north end of York Station in April, 1932, with 'The Flying Scotsman' train from Edinburgh to London. The LNER had just announced that this service and certain others would be 30 to 45 minutes faster from the following month with the scrapping of an agreement, dating from 1895, with their West Coast rivals that 'no train would be faster than eight hours between Edinburgh and London'. Purists will no doubt argue that the headboard was missing a 'The' prefix. *Neg.No.RAIL 25*

Bruce No Knockout

C.Lockhart

IN 1913 I started work as an apprentice locomotive fitter and turner in the Great Central Railway Plant Works at Tuxford, North Nottinghamshire.

Tuxford was only a small place but it was remarkable in that it had, at that time, four railway stations. Now they are all closed.

After being moved several times and suffering a period of unemployment, I returned to Tuxford but the Plant Works there closed in 1926 and I was transferred to Doncaster Plant Works where, after a few years, I became one of 12 charge locomotive erectors, each of which was expected to complete one general repair to one engine per week with a workforce of 24-30 men.

Discipline was strict and manual workers were treated with scant respect. But World War Two changed things when the Essential Works Order became operative and skilled men could not leave the railway, or be easily discharged.

Among my apprentices, I had a lad called Bruce Woodcock who was a very efficient worker who gave no trouble. He was also a boxer of considerable ability and he surprised me one morning when he told me he was not going to do any more work for me as he could not risk damaging his hands. Boxing was more profitable than repairing engines, he said.

This was a problem to me due to the somewhat unusual way of paying locomotive erectors. All the men who worked with me drew their pay from my account, which was made up of previously-agreed contract prices for the locomotives I repaired.

However, the Works Manager, Mr Eggleshaw, kindly intervened. Bruce was transferred to a less hazardous job where he could carry on until he could leave the railway to concentrate on a highly-successful boxing career.

Mr Lockhart lives at Braithwell, Rotherham

Coming in the other way …Class A1 No.60122 'Curlew', sadly minus the all-important headboard, eases 'The Flying Scotsman' train into York from the south on a sunny winter's day — December 29, 1952. *Neg.No.7/C677*

On the right, Class A1 No.60150 'Wilbrook', fitted with early stove pipe chimney, is coming into York Station at a steady pace, overtaking what appears to be a B1 in the distance and, in the left near foreground, D49 'Hunt' Class No.62753 'The Belvoir'. *Neg.No.10/C677*

Apart from the thrill of watching passing steam trains, enthusiasts gained pleasure from the familiarity of locomotives whose home base was York. Here is B16 No.61426, due to go on duty at 2.15pm according to the chalked note on the buffer, easing its way across the web of tracks at York shed. December 29, 1952. *Neg.No.9/C677*

Looking vaguely like a pool full of steaming hippos, although somewhat more orderly, the yard at York shed was near to overflowing with locomotives due to a strike in May, 1949. With around 60 'steamers' on view, it was enough to make any enthusiast weep, for most of their numbers were hidden from this viewpoint. *Neg.No.9/161/K*

Memories are made of this! Countless servicemen must have passed through York over the years, particularly members of the Royal Air Force and Royal Canadian Air Force, both of which had many bases across the Plain of York. In the foreground, a group of them gather at a 'Meeting Point' on one of the station's busy platforms in February, 1948. *Neg.No.RAIL 10*

Steaming Over Smoke Break

Francis Peacock

BACK in 1959, I was based at Ardsley Motive Power Depot. One particular dark night my driver, guard and I were working a goods train back to Wellington Street, Leeds: namely the 20.45hrs ex-Kings Cross. We had been lodging at Kentish Town after working to London from Leeds the previous night.

At approximately 20.15hrs, we backed on to the train and the head shunter connected the coupling and brake pipe. The guard then made his examination, walking around the 50 or 60 wagons, and this took about 20 minutes. When we were satisfied that he was back in his brake van we departed.

We had been going for about half a mile and were in the notorious Gas Works Tunnel, when suddenly, our vacuum brake was lost and we came to a stop.

Neither the driver nor I could see what was wrong through the smoke and steam-filled tunnel, so he asked me to walk back to the rear end.

As I emerged from the tunnel, I saw the guard calmly climbing back into his brake.

When I queried what the trouble was, his reply was to the effect that he had left his Woodbines (cigarettes) in the Kings Cross shunters' cabin and he had been to collect them.

He held them up and I was so furious I could have knocked them out of his hand.

Both the driver and I were smokers but, much as we enjoyed our fags, there is a limit to the inconvenience and delay you should cause to others; especially in such circumstances. Meanwhile, I had to make my way back up the gradient of that filthy tunnel and explain the situation to the driver. As Queen Victoria might have said: he was not amused.

Mr Peacock lives at Pinfold Mount, Whitkirk, Leeds.

Tunnels Come, Tunnels Go...

PROBABLY because of a falling-of of interest in railways among the young, referred to elsewhere in this publication, tunnels no longer hold quite the fascination that they did, say 60 years ago.

In those days, many a 12-year-old could reel off the lengths of Britain's principal tunnels and no serious all-embracing book on railways was complete without reference to the engineering feats which had gone into the large bores which often cut miles off routes the lines would otherwise have had to follow. More recently, tunnels of incredible lengths have been completed and the engineering equipment and skills have been vastly up-rated to make them possible.

Tunnelling always was, and still is, a dangerous occupation and the loss of life involved over the years has been considerable. All this probably led to the fact that much of the work, in various countries, was mainly done by foreign labour imported specially for the job at rates that were not attractive to the locals, considering the dangers. In America and Canada it was Chinese labour which bore the brunt of much tunnelling work; in Britain, Irish navvies were prominent in the task.

With small boys operating toy trains, three books — one on each side of the line opened-up like an 'A' frame, the third laid across their spines was enough to make a 'tunnel' until enough pocket money was saved or a birthday present made the purchase of a manufactured tunnel possible.

Railway architecture in Britain was generally pleasing and substantial: practically all tunnel mouths were given an acceptable look with cut stone trimmings — and often quite elaborate (as at Bramhope Tunnel between Leeds and Harrogate) to satisfy land-owners across whose property the railways had been allowed to proceed.

in North America, the builders began with similar good intent in the older eastern states, but as the great race developed to open-up the West, such attention to detail was forgotten as a plentiful supply of timber, oft-near at hand, made massive wooden abutments possible; or in the mountains tunnels which had been blasted through rock were often left with mouths no better than those of caves. But with the coming of concrete, some were given the benefit of a smooth facing; often with the date of construction set above the tunnel mouth.

There used to be a World War One saying which has been altered to fit various situations, but was most popular as: 'If you can find a better hole, go and get one.' Well, in terms of the North of England, with the massive Pennine Chain splitting the eastern and western halves of the country, there was no better hole than the Standedge Tunnel between Yorkshire and Lancashire.

In fact, there were three — two older, single line tunnels, and the present twin-track bore,

which was completed in 1894, running three miles and 64 yards between Marsden in the north-east and Diggle in the south-west.

Generations of local railwaymen knew this third tunnel as the 'Slow up and down'. It also had a nickname — 'Pots and Pans' — and today it carries all the traffic. The two older tunnels, which had been known as 'Fast up' and 'Fast down', were closed by British Railways in 1966.

The way the brooding Pennines 'split' the weath-

er at Standedge has long fascinated travellers through the tunnel. On eastbound trains it is not unusual to leave the (now) Lancashire side bathed in bright sunlight, then arrive in Yorkshire under glowering skies and pouring rain. On other days, a similar split could occur when travelling westbound.

Here is the entrance at Marsden with a train in the tunnel mouth on the left. Almost immediately below it is the entrance to the canal tunnel. *Neg.N/A.*

This close-up view of Standedge's Yorkshire portal clearly shows the bridge just ahead of the tunnel mouth. To the right the canal tunnel entrance of 1811 was protected by gates when this picture was taken in November, 1976. Old bargees told fascinating tales of lying on their backs on the hold covers of their narrow boats, 'walking on the roof' to propel their boats through the Pennines. *Neg.N/A*

Of the millions of passengers who travelled through the old single bore tunnels at Standedge over the years, few knew about 'The Cathedral' area. This was the nickname given to part of the structure by the railway gangs to a section which adjoined the old twin bores about half-way through their length. This picture, taken in November, 1966, shows Inspector H. Hanson and Works Inspector Percy Richardson studying a section of 'The Cathedral'. Serious faults in the strata, compression problems and the results of poor workmanship were among the reasons for this reinforcement.

Less well-known is why the railwaymen gave the nickname 'Pots and Pans' to the new double-line tunnel. However, it is generally believed today that it came from a primitive warning device which had been rigged up to warn workers outside the tunnel entrance that the train was on its way. A veteran railwayman reports that a metal plate alongside one of the lines was struck by the wheel flanges of the engine, and its coaches/wagons. In turn, this actuated a set of rods which caused a gong to be struck. This might well have been the 'banging and clanking' sound which quite a lot of steam era travellers recall hearing just before their trains left Standedge. *Neg.N/A*

The dangers of intruders, particularly children, venturing on to railway property is no better illustrated than in this picture, deep underground in 'The Cathedral' area, where exponents of graffiti had left their mark on the tunnel walls, long after the track had been lifted. Structural engineer Mr Graham Sykes was inspecting 'The Cathedral' arches when this photograph was taken. *Neg.N/A*

Broomhouse Tunnel, between Sheffield and Chesterfield, was 'a bit of a conundrum' as the locals would have it. With a length of only 92 yards, and not exactly a mountain on top of it, one might have felt that it would have been cheaper to continue the cutting right through, instead of cutting a bore and then building substantial tunnel entrances. It seems that thought came to someone in 1969 — 100 years after the tunnel was made — when it appears that landslips were causing problems and this ugly fence of old sleepers was built to try and keep debris from reaching the lines. *Neg.N/A*

The end came for Broomhouse in August, 1969. Explosives were set so that the sides would cave in and the roof fall without far-flying debris. This picture shows the moment of truth when the tunnel literally burst open then fell back into the pit. The operation was highly successful, a railway spokesman said later. *Picture: White's, Sheffield.*

Of all the tunnelling projects which accompanied the growth of railways in Britain, few gained such an infamous reputation as Woodhead, half-way between Sheffield and Manchester in a particularly bleak and cheerless section of the Pennines.

Two tunnels were bored between between 1839 and 1852, and were just over three miles long, linking Woodhead in Cheshire with Dunford Bridge in Yorkshire. The first, once the longest tunnel seen in Britain, was built between 1839 and 1845. Of the hundreds of hard-drinking navvies who lived and worked in squalor on the site, 32 were killed and 140 received serious injuries.

The second bore was blasted alongside in the years 1847 to 1852. Hazards were fewer and conditions less distressing, but an outbreak of cholera claimed 28 of the 70 men burrowing beneath the moors on a round-the-clock rota.

This picture shows the imposing portals of the tunnels at Woodhead.

They were not used for rail traffic after 1954, following the start of a cleaning operation by the Central Electricity Generating Board which spent £2,750,000 converting one of them to take transmission cables under the Pennine Ridge at Bleakow Moor. *Neg.N/A*

This special rig was erected on its own lines at the Dunford Bridge end of the tunnel to handle the outsize drums on which the five-inch cables were wound. They were designed to carry up to 4,000,000 kilowatts at peak loading. So much heat was created by this that troughs of water were installed through the length of the tunnel to cool them. The water flowed from Dunford to Woodhead, and was then pumped back again for re-use. Power was carried from Ferrybridge power station to Stalybridge, and from Eggborough to the Midlands. But the tunnels had not seen the last of 'railway' traffic: a narrow gauge line was laid alongside the cable troughs to enable maintenance to be carried out quickly. *Neg.N/A*

Meanwhile, 'real' trains continued to run under the Pennines and still do, via the Woodhead New Tunnel which was opened on June 3, 1954, by the Rt Hon Alan Lennox-Boyd, Minister of Transport and Aviation, pictured here with a plaque marking the occasion. *Neg.N/A*

The London Underground and a few other short tunnels apart, few people would associate city centres as venues for 'real' tunnels such as bore through cliffs and mountains. Yet the claim for the first passenger railway tunnel in Britain is made for one almost within a stone's throw of Leeds Parish Church.

In 1834 the Leeds & Selby Railway beat several other emergent railway companies to win what would no doubt today be called 'the dash for downtown Leeds'. First promoted in 1829, the L&S was the first passenger railway in the West Riding, although its terminus hardly reached the city centre proper. It was located in the then dirtiest part of the city at Marsh Lane.

That notorious spot lay considerably below the green uplands to the east of the city and Marsh Lane Cutting had to be dug and blasted to provide a gradient which the early locomotives could tackle in safety. Near the bottom of the cutting, a tunnel was dug through Richmond Hill and for Leeds 'Loiners', as local residents were known, it became one of the wonders of the world.

Not all of them were overjoyed at its appearance: many were as wary about travelling underground as are some of them today in relation to the Channel Tunnel. Eventually, to alleviate their fears, the railway's directors had sheets of polished copper hung under the ventilation shafts to re-direct daylight into the tunnel. In addition, some sections of the tunnel walls were whitewashed but such 'improvements' did little for passengers who sat near-choking in open wagons.

In due course the tunnel was opened up and the cutting widened to accommodate four tracks where, as can be seen in this picture, the still substantial gradient was being tackled by Class B9 No.61475 with a mixture of LNER stock on November 15, 1951. *Neg.5/C603*

A Signal Affair

FROM the earliest days of railways, it quickly became clear that some form of external control was required if footplate crews were (a) to be able to propel their engines safely through the countryside and, more importantly, busy urban areas; (b) to be protected themselves from errors which they, or like crews, might make; and (c) to be able to conduct their trains on their lawful occasions, getting the best out of them, but again without risk to others — especially passengers.

Of all the railway infrastructure involved in safety of operation, little was more evident, easily-recognised and well-known to the public at large than the signals; whether they be lonely single posts on quiet branch lines or the giant gantries whose ranks of posts rose and fell in order of importance across the approaches to stations like Waterloo, Paddington and other major termini.

Thinking back about the latter, and having spent some years commuting into Central London from its suburbs in the days when 'pea-souper' fogs were a menace to life and limb and health in general, the compiler of this book is still full of admiration for the footplate crews and signalmen who had the training, discipline, expertise and confidence to guide iron steeds under a forest of signal posts and over a mesh of trackwork in unerring fashion, year in, year out. Here, in order of importance, are some examples of what they faced in terms of signals.

A somewhat stunted signal, part of which looks as if it might have been held together by bits of Meccano, guards a siding at Stourton, Leeds, as 'Jubilee' Class 45675 'Hardy' leaves a clean white vapour trail at the head of a London-Newcastle express on April 22, 1953. *Neg.No.2/C695*

Those Were The Days...

Graham G.Kennewell

AT the age of 87 I reminisce on my experiences, first as apprentice fitter/turner with the Hull & Barnsley Railway, then, after the 1921 takeover with the NER.

When I started on 12 April 1920, H&B's Chief Engineer was Matthew Stirling, son of the famous Patrick Stirling of the GNR Doncaster.

There were then no paid holidays for H&B shop staff, only footplate and clerical grades. Apprentices were allowed five Bank Holidays with pay, plus (an ancient custom) Shrove Tuesday afternoon. Being the last apprentice taken on by the H&B, I benefited from this practice until I was 21.

Having gone through all stages of training, and studying (at my own expense) at night school three nights a week to gain the National Certificate of Engineers and the SI Mech E qualifications, I became a journeyman earning £2 12s a week.

It was customary on the man's 21st birthday to present particular colleagues with cigars, to parade through workshops, and, at noon, accompanied by loud drumming on any handy object, to depart on a precious half-day holiday.

There were characters a-plenty amongst one's fellow workers. The man, for instance, who chewed 8oz of Pigtail Tobacco a week, never smoked, and could hit a sixpence at a distance of five feet with his cud!

Many men had nicknames, and one driver I remember at Dairycoates Shed earned his when his engine was all ready prepared for going out. The fireman called the driver to come on to the turntable. He opened the regulator, but instead of going forward, the engine went backwards straight through the shed wall.

On being asked for an explanation by the Superintendent he replied: "She just give yah puff and went right through t'wall." From that day on he was known as 'Ya Puff'.

Mr Kennewell is a retired Mechanical Foreman of the York Running Shed (now the National Railway Museum). He lives at Sheriff Hutton, York.

The signalman and his lad in Marsh Lane box, Leeds, could almost reach out and change their gantry signals by hand, as they posed in 'Over the garden wall' style. As for the rest ...'and the shunters engaged the driver in earnest conversation' as they might have said in a Buckingham Palace garden party picture (or something like that). It was a quiet moment at Marsh Lane and the five railway employees were more likely interested in what the photographer was up to. The Class J7 vintage 1899 tank's steam dome looked as if it had enjoyed a mass attack by inner city pigeons, or else Leeds water disagreed with it. There were enough fire irons, shovels, buckets and what-have-you on the nearside water tank to see the fireman through any task: especially frying bacon between bouts of shunting. *Neg.No.8/C604*

A larger size of semaphore oversees the progress of 'Hunt' Class 'The Cottesmore' (No.62749) as its somewhat curious Lentz Rotary Cam poppet valve equipment propels it through Holbeck on November 22, 1951. *Neg.No.5/C605*

Clanking engine, clanking points, the unmistakable sound of a 'falling' signal; point rodding and signal wires everywhere. This magnificent array of vintage signals and other railway infrastructure and rolling stock, underlines the wonder of the uninitiated as to how footplate crews knew which signal was set for them as smoke and steam swirled around on a murky night. York-based V2 No.60843 passes Neville Hill with a Newcastle-Leeds train in May, 1953. Since then, signals, locomotive and probably all the rolling stock in sight have been scrapped. *Neg.No.2/C698*

Taking A General View

TIME was when the 'spotter' with more individual tastes (and even more so the photographer), would have his favourite viewing spot which provided a general view of the maximum amount of railway activity.

Not for them the heaving and pushing on platform ends where the photographers, especially, were hard-pressed to be able to assess the situation, let alone get a decent view, or even hold a camera still long enough to click the shutter.

The many wide open spaces of railway property in industrial and suburban areas were often ideal for the specialist ...as these general views reveal:

Where have all those chimneys gone? The Leeds skyline has changed almost beyond recognition since this picture was snapped of A3 No.60055 'Woolwinder', gleaming in the sun as it headed for London with the 3.25pm express on August 1, 1952. *Neg.No.2/C651*

Heroic Act Went Unrecognised

J.H.Hirst

I WAS working on the night shift as a Train Register Boy at Mexborough No 1 Signal-box in 1952.

Working with me was Signalman C.S. (Charlie) Fisher, a very experienced rail-wayman.

At about 03.00hrs Charlie sprang from his chair having heard a faint tooting sound which turned out to be the driver of a heavily-loaded Ashwell to Frodingham iron ore train warning that the train was running away out of control down the incline from Swinden Junction.

Charlie, showing commendable calmness, proceeded to switch the junction points to allow the runaway train to run over the main line towards Cadeby instead of diverting it into the goods line.

This action undoubtedly saved the life of the guard of a goods train which was standing on the goods line at the time.

I shall never forget the sparks showering from the brakes of the iron ore train engine as the runaway train thundered past the signalbox, the driver and fireman having baled out further down the line, fortunately suffering no injuries.

I have to say that in over 40 years' railway service, which included spells as Station Manager in various parts of the country and as Deputy Chief Controller at Eastern Region HQ York, I never witnessed an emergency situation dealt with more calmly and efficiently than this was by Charlie Fisher.

Sadly, it was never officially recognised by the management at the time.

Charlie was over 50 years of age at the time of the incident and I lost contact with him when I left to do my National Service. I salute his memory.

Mr Hirst lives at Bradwell Avenue, Dodworth, Barnsley

Take the smoke and steam out of this picture and you could almost be looking at a typical 00-gauge layout at any model railway show these days, for the amount of detail put into lineside features and background is often quite astonishing. But put the steam, the clanking and the clickety-clack back into it and you have the real, life-size Engine Shed Junction, down in south Leeds, with Class 5F No,42851 in the foreground and No.73138 with the 'nationalised wheel' on its tender cutting across to the right. *Neg.No.H/786/6*

In full cry — 'Hunt' Class No.62745 'The Hurworth' heads down into Leeds from the North-East on April 20, 1951, through a vast amount of railway infrastructure shooting off in all directions. *Neg.No.6/C604*

Just how much commercial and industrial progress, recessions, closures and general changes have altered the Leeds area's skyline comes to light when this picture is magnified several times and it is clear that a whole clutter of industrial chimneys has vanished for ever. And so has much of what we see in the foreground where two tank engines are engaged on shunting duties whilst an 'Austerity' heavy goods engine lurks under the bridge on the right. The tank in the foreground, 0-6-0 No.47567, is one of a class developed by the LMS from an earlier Midland Railway design. The location is Wortley, Leeds. *Neg.No.C940/1*

Not exactly for the frenzied activity railway fan, but well-suited to the title 'Classic Steam' — it's a glorious day as 'The Thames-Clyde Express', hauled by No.45597, snakes through the high country of Dentdale. Note the viaduct in the far distance — just above and to the right of the loco's chimney. *Neg.No.7/C710*

Closer, perhaps, to the real 'rivet-counter's' heart than the last idyllic scene: there's smoke, steam, soot and general 'clag' everywhere as a shunting engine gasps from underneath the bridge to part-ly cloud the photographer's view of A1 No.60139 'Sea Eagle' as it hauls 'The Queen of Scots' through Wortley, Leeds. No doubt there would be those aboard the Pullman thinking that, all things con-sidered looking through the curtain-bordered windows, they would prefer to be in the Highlands or the Home Counties. *Neg.No.12/C596*

STEAM TALES

All Puffed Up On The Scarborough Flyer

Maurice Batty

IT was a Saturday morning in the summer of 1950. My mate, (driver) Walter Hardy and I were waiting in Sheffield Station with a B16 4-6-0 engine for an excursion train which we were going to take on to Scarborough. It was a half hour late arriving.

The Stanier 'Black Five' engine was un-coupled from its coaches and then we backed on to them. Whilst I was coupling up, Walter was laughing and joking with the passengers. They were moaning about being late but Walter told them they had been on the 'Let Me Sleep' railway (LMS), but now they were with the LNER and we would have them in Scarborough on time.

With a full head of steam we were bristling to go. With passengers on board and a green flag we were off.

The B16 was making light work of the 16 coaches, roaring past Mexborough, Pon-tefract, Burton Salmon, Church Fenton and Copmanthorpe. Approaching York, signals gave us caution and we dropped our speed going into York station; with a good red fire in the box, as no smoke was allowed going through the station. York was bursting at the seams with holiday passengers. We got the green signal: all clear ahead!

Walter had an audience: he opened the regulator, the wheels were slipping; then the engine barked like an angry dragon, spitting red hot sparks. Our passengers hung out of the windows shouting Walter on. We whizzed through Malton and ar-rived at Scarborough five minutes early!

Walter was soon on the platform with his chest stuck out. Our passengers thought he was a hero, slapping him on his back and shaking his hand.

But the following week found Walter and I hauled over the coals; passengers on the platform at York had put in hundreds of pounds' worth of claims for burnt clothing! Egos deflated, Walter got one week's sus-pension with caution and I got three days with a caution.

Mr Batty was employed at Selby Loco Sheds from 1943 to 1954.

Friendly and Familiar — The B1 Class

EACH of the 'Big Four' railways had engines which were as friendly and familiar to passengers 'as a greengrocer's whistle' as the saying went in the days when greengrocers had something to whistle about.

Not for them thunderous starts from Kings Cross to tackle early gradients; or the exhilaration of hurtling down the bank to go through Retford; accompanied by the electrifying sound of a chime whistle, with bits of litter dancing between the sleepers in their wake.

No — these were modest, adaptable machines that made good time with stopping trains, or hauled excursions to the coast, or ran out from the cities to moderately-sized towns (the word 'intercity' had not yet been invented). But they were important in their own way, and could be seen in numbers in the London area, especially at Liverpool Street.

Typical were the members of the LNER's B1 Class of sturdy 4-6-0s which looked solid and reliable. The originals were built at the company's Darlington Works, others were constructed in Glasgow by the North British Locomotive Company whose products used to be sold all over the world.

Brought into service as late as 1942, the B1s weighed 71 tons 3cwts (tender 52 tons) and had 6ft 2ins driving wheels. Ample kit to pound happily across the Plain of York and through the delights of the East Riding in late summer for a day out at Scarborough.

'Lord Balfour of Burleigh' B1 No.61246 in impressively clean condition at Copley Hill, Leeds, on August 2, 1951. *Neg.No.25/C652*

Also at Copley Hill, the same day, was 61033 'Dibatag', simmering gently as it awaited the call to duty. *Neg.No.24/C652*

This picture of B1 No.61020 'Gemsbok' is often mistaken for that which appeared on the front page of Volume One in the original set of 'pocket' volumes of *Yorkshire Steam Collection* pictures, published some 20 years ago. Not so! The engine on the cover wasn't a B1, it was B16/2 No.61475 and it was chucking out a fair amount of poorly-burned coal dust and general clag. However, those who were confused have one slight consolation: the rake of coaches behind this B1 is almost certainly the same set which appeared behind the engine on the cover. Both were pictured at Marsh Lane, Leeds, the one above on November 10, 1951. *Neg.No.7/C604*

No.61216 was leaving Arthington for Harrogate and Northallerton on a February day in 1957, with either a fresh-air fanatic or a heavy smoker behind the half-open window in the second compartment from the front. *Neg.No.BIW40*

With coaches no doubt well-filled with shoppers eager to explore what has long been reputed as the best shopping centre in the North, 61256 was making easy work of the run through Killingbeck and the Leeds eastern suburbs on its way down to City Station with a train from York on May 8, 1953. *Neg.No.3/C698*

"'ello, wot's this box on wheels, then?" B1 No.61165 looks as if it might possibly be sniffing at the newcomer's intrusion as two eras met in January, 1952. The electric Class EM1 No.26026 was built for the electrified Wath-Sheffield-Manchester line but, thanks to lack of foresight all-round, the life of this environmentally-friendly system was short-lived. *Neg.No.3/762R*

Clanking its lonely way home, 61016 'Inyala' hardly looks like a winner on the four track 'racetrack' north of York. December 6, 1955. *Neg.No.9/C886*

Clear As Black & White

DESPITE the incredible advances in the quality of, and results from, colour film, there are still photographers — not least among railway enthusiasts, who feel that monochrome brings out best results for them.

Always a matter of opinion, of course, and when the great majority of pictures in this book were taken, the photographers concerned were limited to 'black and white'. In some respects, their pictures brought out the 'warts and all' aspects of the steam age, for however one loved 'live steam' some would always proclaim it 'dead dirty'. As if that mattered! Most young lads would have risked a telling-off anytime in return for half-an-hour on a footplate, with a crew more likely to say, 'A little bit of muck never did anybody any harm,' rather than, 'Don't get your hands dirty.' Here are four test samples of whiter than white, blacker than black, and more hot water than a fussy mother could ever want in her 'set-pot' boiler…

Begrimed B1 No.61218, 'mucked up' apart from tiny reflections on its steam dome, chimney and well-oiled rods, runs into Leeds City with a Bradford to Hull train. *Neg.No.3/C594*

Straight lines, smooth curves and circles …steam, oil, grease, ashes, grit and grime …it's a far cry from the prim interior of a Pullman car as streamlined A4 No.60029, which eventually took the name 'Woodcock' planned for a predecessor, simmers 'on shed' at Copley Hill, Leeds, on August 1, 1952. On the right, easing its way alongside, is A1 No.60141 'Abbotsford'. Other technology of the period takes the form of a wheelbarrow — with a rubber tyre! *Neg.No.1/C651*

An interesting play on light and dark as a train of aged non-corridor coaches, drawn by 2-6-2 tank No.40090, enters Holbeck (Low Level) Station with a Leeds-Ilkley train on November 2, 1951. Note the entrance/exit for the subway on the right.

In view of the IRA bomb damage done to modern signalling equipment boxes outside Leeds Station at the time of writing, one wonders what chance the wooden boxes and the 'Fog Hut' on the left would have had in the event of such an attack!

Also note the curious signal gantry and telephone pole arrangement just to the left of the locomotive's chimney. *Neg.No.7/C605*

Always trained to get the facts, the *Yorkshire Post* photographer who took this atmospheric study of the interior of Leeds City Station, on a sunny day in the early 1950s, was moved to note that in the

gloom on the right, ex-LMS 'Jubilee' Class No.45608 'Gibraltar' was simmering quietly, whilst on the left former LNER B1 No.61218 was contributing a considerable amount of smoke to the

general railway atmosphere and charm of 'City' which, in those days, looked as if it had actually suffered bomb damage! *Neg.No.C940/5*

Marshalling Yards

ASK THE average Internet-wise youngster what he knows about marshalling yards and you might as well ask him if he's ever operated a crystal set.

Yet like the now near-forgotten bomber stations of World War Two, railway marshalling yards once covered huge sites around Britain. Coincidentally, those of the German railways were a favourite target of the RAF's Bomber Command.

In simple terms for the uninitiated, marshalling yards were places where railway wagons were sorted out and made up into trains.

A feature of most of the larger ones was the 'hump' where trains of wagons to be sorted were pushed up an incline, uncoupled as required, then allowed to run forward by gravity down to the lines where trains were made up.

Marshalling yards still exist in Britain, of course, but the amount of traffic using them is nothing like it was in the heyday of steam. For one thing, the wagons tend to be larger, so fewer movements are required and, sadly, lack of a co-ordinated transport policy in Britain has tended to allow road hauliers to run away with much of what used to be rail-borne traffic.

Whether Britain's newly-privatised railway companies have the will, desire or the know-how to recapture the trade is a matter of opinion. What is a matter of fact is that with traffic-jammed roads becoming an everyday occurrence, manufacturers, especially exporters, might well be forced into a rethink and put their traffic back on the railway.

American railroads are years ahead in moving freight traffic and giant marshalling yards and container bases, many several miles in length, are busy night and day handling a boom in business.

Sign of the times: this was the scene in September, 1969, at the disused freight marshalling yard at Normanton, where only a few rusting wagons served as a reminder of the time when the constant clatter of buffers filled the air. The yard was closed as a part of the general rundown of the railway industry at Normanton, once one of the most important rail centres in the North. Around the same time, the marshalling yards at Hunslet and Stourton, Leeds, were also closed and goods traffic bound for Leeds and surrounding districts had to be taken to Healey Mills, at the other side of Wakefield, for sorting and then brought back by local trip trains. *Neg.N/A*

Sign of the old times — when coal was king, the Normanton yard would have looked more like it does in this picture. Now all the wagons have gone — and so have all the lines shown here and those in the previous picture, other than the through-running lines. *Neg.N/A*

There were still great hopes for railway freight traffic when the new Tees Marshalling Yard (pictured) was opened in May, 1963. These are the 'Up' reception sidings, with wagons going 'over the hump' in the foreground and the engine release subway underneath them. *Picture: British Railways North Eastern*

This is the control room at Healey Mills, four miles west of Wakefield, on the one time Lancashire & Yorkshire Railway. Pictured in December, 1964, a year after it opened, the yard was a part of BR's North Eastern Region modernisation plan for moving freight and was the largest in Yorkshire with a capacity to handle 3,000 wagons a day. The tower's operators, at their control panels, were provided with radio telephones to ensure constant communication with yard staff and the crews of shunting engines. *Neg.N/A.*

The North Eastern Region's modernisation plan had obviously not got down to Wellington Street, Leeds, by 1968. There, in a building with a sign which read: 'London Midland and Scottish Railway, Orders for Delivery' (the LMS had been delivered up to nationalisation some 20 years before), clerks were working under the incandescent mantles of gas lights, as here. But Cellophane had been invented and covered instructions which had been taped to the walls. And to speed freight its way, a poster ex-

horted employees to send freight to the right depot! One wonders if that had anything to do with BR's already falling share of the freight market. *Neg.N/A*

Making Tracks — An Epic Story

MENTION Railtrack in any gathering of railway enthusiasts and controversy is almost sure to spill out like an over-filled tender. But, despite the arguments on that score, no one can deny that whatever happens in the next few years, Britain's railways will never again be of a size that reflected the sheer exuberance of those who set out to build the finest railway system in the world.

The lines were everywhere, up hill and down dale, across the Fens, climbing mountains, skirting the sea, meshing through south London like a collection of huge scissors dropped by a giant, sloping through Lincolnshire and emerging all mucky into Manchester.

They were well-laid and well-maintained by proud and proper men who scorned American claims to have laid longer sections of track in one day than anyone else. "Aye, but will t'trains stay on 'em?" would be the sort of comment raised on the GNR, or the Midland, or Great Western.

It was a well put question, for a whole series of major and minor disasters followed the American and Canadian rush to link both sides of the North American continent. Nevertheless, it was a mighty achievement and in due course American know-how developed a weight of track that was strong enough to carry the world's largest locomotives, capable of hauling loads undreamt of in the land that invented the steam engine; and so big many could not have been fitted into UK tunnels.

But the pride of the British 'lengthmen' was justified because Britain was long at the top of the rail safety league and visitors from Canada, Australia and the US were amazed to see British track workers 'lining up' the edges of the ballast so that everything was neat and tidy and as good-looking as the countryside through which the trains ran with stylish and often pristine appearance.

When those lines got to the towns and cities it was, of course, another matter: they spread here and there, were squeezed between factories, ran on viaducts, down steep gradients, through the clashing ironwork of bridges carrying lines that intermeshed at various levels, then eventually escaped into the countryside again.

Small boys might well wonder how the heck somebody sorted it all out. But sort it out they did and their rail tracks were a credit to them, standing up to two world wars, only to be severely wounded by the unfortunate Doctor Beeching — acting on orders.

This assortment of pictures shows British railtracks in their latter heyday. Perhaps that heyday may return when commonsense tells the powers that be that Britain just cannot stand much more road traffic; or when we all decide that seeing as we can't even get out of our own driveways, we'd better dump/sell/mothball the car and start making tracks for the trains.

With surrounding tracks looking as if they could have stitched together earthquake crevices, A2 Class No.60502 'Earl Marischal', a rebuild of an earlier design, steams out of York in the December sunshine of 1952. *Neg.No.1/C677*

For years, pictures like this of the north end of Newcastle upon Tyne Station have appeared in scores of publications. In the south, the tracks out of Waterloo Station held a similar fascination. Those who think of railways as 'old-fashioned' might do well to bear in mind that, yes, trackwork like this has been round for over a century, but a system that was good for trains then is good for trains being built today. Will the same claim be able to be made for the aviation industry's jet planes, only just over half a century into their history, if they reach a 'hundred up' around 2040? One doubts it, especially considering that stage coaches were early rivals of the railways.

Most fathers who have attempted to put together the lines of comparatively simple model railway sets on Christmas mornings over the years will, no doubt, agree that the railway builders were a remarkable lot. The driver of Don-caster-built (in 1925) A3 Pacific 60060 'The Tetrarch' certainly had every confidence in them as his mount allowed itself to be guided out of Newcastle by their handiwork with a parcels train for Scotland in November, 1951. *Neg.No.1/570R*

Transition curves, curves within curves, a diamond (or 'flat') crossing for good measure — they were all still in place at York on December 29, 1952, as track workers stood clear to allow the passing of a grime-coated 'St Mungo' (A1 No.60145). There was no headboard to reveal that this was the southbound 'The Flying Scotsman' train (a near Hogmanay safety precaution against souvenir hunters, perhaps?) en route from Edinburgh to London. But the coaches still carry name boards for a once-proud train. *Neg.No.6/C677*

There's a fair thrashing of points, plus a couple of old wooden vans that many an LNER enthusiast would like to model, in this pre-World War Two picture of the LNER's classic 'Pacific' 'Sir Nigel Gresley' (it seems hardly necessary to give its number — 4498) as it leans into a suburban curve, gathering speed. The Doncaster-built engine was named after its designer and is lovingly preserved. The compiler of this publication has proudly told his grandsons: "I once blew the chime whistle on that engine!" *Neg.No.5/C681*

One of the signalmen eyes the photographer across a welter of lines as ex-LMS No.45078 moves slowly past Neville Hill West Box, Leeds. Sturdy signal posts and a 16-crossbar telephone pole are a reminder of the days when things were 'built to last'. *Neg.No.9/C604*

Surely that crouching lengthman can't be using a spirit level? Or *were* they that keen? A Wortley, Leeds, signalman's eye view of the area's mass of trackwork and 'The Queen of Scots Pullman' headed by A1 No.60116 'Hal O' The Wynd' in the days when Leeds was a train spotter's joy. October 4, 1951. *Neg.No.12/C593*

A bit of snakelike work here: points, point rodding, point levers and signal wires are everywhere at the bottom of Marsh Lane Cutting, Leeds, as B1 No.61071 coasts down to City Station with a train from Scarborough on November 15, 1951. *Neg.No.3/C603*

In today's world of railways, the name of Southport hardly raises a thrill among the enthusiasts, but time was when Lancashire's 'posher' resort attracted sufficient visitors to require a good deal of rail trackage in and around its station. Venturing cautiously into Red Rose territory, the photographer managed to capture Class 3P 2-6-2 tank No.40192 heading 'em out for Preston in 1956. The clue to the amount of track variety at any station was, of course, the number of signals; and there is no shortage of them in this picture. August, 1956. *Neg.No.BIW9*

This fascinating picture of Wortley Junction, Leeds, raised much comment when it appeared in the Autumn/Winter 1996 edition of *Portraits of Steam.*. It was taken by Ernest Mayes, a long-time signalman, in 1951 when he was doing his period of service at 'The Junction' and the accompanying article by Peter Rose included tributes to Ernest's skill at capturing fascinating slices of railway life on film, and his pride in the railway system; the latter being underlined by this picture. Few people under 50 will remember the enormous amount of railway property in Leeds, especially south of the River Aire. There are, for instance, over 20 tracks across the width of this picture; today there are a handful. Ernest took the shot from a precarious position on the gantry of the 'Down' fast line signal. On the left was the big but now long-gone gasworks and its sidings on the western edge of what is now the 'Armley Gyratory' which figures daily in rush hour traffic reports on local radio. Also on the is the left signal box where Ernest was working at that time. To the right are sidings alongside the then main A647 road up to Armley. Various car sales and other companies now stand on that site and retail outlets have replaced most of the property on the far right. What is left includes the main running lines out to the Aire Valley and the Hosforth/Harrogate branch via Kirkstall Viaduct.

Sadly, Ernest passed away on January 23, 1997, before we reproduced another set of his pictures in *Portraits of Steam*. This much-respected railwayman will be much missed and we wish to thank his widow, Elsie, for permission to use this picture of 'The Junction'.

Getting Enthusiastic

IF YOU think that it is only in the 1990s (possibly having been set the example by Aussie schoolchildren in 'soaps' from Down Under) that youngsters are in the habit of sitting around on the ground creating inconvenience for adults, then think again. And don't imagine that juveniles roaming across rail lines is a new experience.

This picture appeared in the *Yorkshire Post* on April 21, 1960, along with a story which read: 'Hundreds of train spotters, crowding platforms and buffets, running across the tracks, hanging from footbridges and throwing things on the lines are causing mounting anxiety for Doncaster Station staff.

'As a result, a conference has been called at the station, which is a major mecca for spotters, and Mr Joe Walsh, the stationmaster, is inviting suggestions from his staff on how to cope with the problem.' (What a pity we are not privy to all they suggested!)

The story went on to say that children from far afield homed-in on Doncaster because there was so much rail activity, and on some days more than a thousand boys were 'hanging about' (hopefully not from footbridges).

Possibly the most useful suggestion to come from the staff was the possibility of having 'pens' in various sections of the platforms. Strangely enough, many airports have, over the years, cashed-in on similar schemes for aviation fans. They have proved to be nice little earners and near-eliminated previous problems.

Over the past few years, however, there has been a general feeling regarding a falling-off of interest in railways, particularly among the young. Perhaps British railways in general have had so much bad publicity that children are turned-off any useful association with them.

They are, of course, an easy target for vandals; but that is an international problem and touches every aspect of society.

Preserved railways have done, and continue to do, a magnificent job in keeping interest alive but ever-rising costs, especially in the areas of insurance and maintenance (steam locomotives are notoriously expensive to maintain) are a threat to keeping them running. So is there a danger of them ending-up as museum pieces, however carefully they have been maintained?

It would be a tragedy if, at a time when rail travel is enjoying a revival in developed countries, and not necessarily because of privatisation, we were unable to pass on some 'live' and tangible evidence of our railway heritage to generations to come.

A picture to wake-up the reader who eats, drinks and sleeps steam: it might not look like an enthusiasts' special but judging by the number of BR personnel on board, and watching from the tracks behind, they were giving an enthusiastic reception to this experimental run of a diesel multiple unit leaving Skipton for Carlisle in January, 1955. The trials were successful and similar trains took over local trains on this route for a period. Then, after a gap of some years, diesel units again appeared under the 'Dalerail' scheme. *Neg.No.RAIL 4*

Ever heard the expression: 'We were crowded like cattle into wagons' …? Well, this lot were not complaining about some BR train. In fact, despite the inclement weather, you can find one or two smiles among this trainload of enthusiasts who braved not only the weather but also the locomotive's exhaust as they trundled along in coal wagons in 1968, for the last steam-hauled journey at Waterloo Main Colliery, Leeds. *Neg.No.RAIL 35*

You can always spot an enthusiasts' special: they are the only trains where there are heads sticking out of the windows even when it's pouring with rain. In charge was LNER 4472 'Flying Scotsman' returning to Steamtown, Carnforth, after attending the 'Rail 150' celebrations in the North East in October, 1975. En route it called at the National Railway Museum, York, so that the more 'way out' fans could actually stroke the engine. Here it is a little further west, snaking its way into Leeds City. The sharp-eyed reader will have noted what appears 'to be an extra tender. In fact it was the tender of No.1306 'Mayflower' also tucked in behind the 'Scotsman'. *Neg.No.RAIL32*

Most of the transport which ventures out of the Humber is bound for the high seas, but 'Black Five' 5305 was well and truly on dry land at Leeds City Station, heading the Humberside Locomotive Society's special, the 'Humber Venturer' in April, 1978. Just look at the polish on this engine — especially the buffers. One thing is certain, whatever stick they have to take from the unthinking chattering classes and cheap gibe comedians, looking at these pictures you realise that railway enthusiasts must have been cherished for years by the manufacturers of film. (Ironically *Neg.N/A!*)

Whether it be in city, town, or countryside, the 'fans', 'buffs' — call them what you will — were and still are out in force if there's a steamer about.

This was a farewell occasion: Railway Correspondence and Travel Society members and friends picture their double-headed special train at

Barnard Castle before it set off over the Pennines by the bleak Stainmore line, then about to be axed. *Neg.No.RAIL 20*

Here's that show-stopper again: celebrating its Diamond Jubilee, the 'Flying Scotsman' was host to the Russell Harty TV show which was recorded as

the engine took a special train from Steamtown to Leeds. The steam mega-star was photographed when it stopped briefly at Skipton where it seemed

half the population was either on the platforms or had overflowed on to the lines. *Neg.N/A*

Whereas enthusiasts from Humberside poured into Leeds on their special, fans from inland poured into Whitby in October, 1987, when 'Evening Star', the last steam locomotive manufactured for British Rail, puffed into town. *Neg.N/A*

Being the largest engine ever to visit Yorkshire's famous fishing port, and being in pristine condition for the occasion, a footplate 'guard' in 'scare 'em off' day-glo jacket was keeping a beady eye out for Whitby's notorious seagulls. *Picture: Philip George*

Then known to many as 'Lord Garnock's engine', and looking as if it might have come straight out of a Hornby box, 'The Great Marquess' was on test at Neville Hill, Leeds, in June, 1966. His Lordship had wisely had the loco restored to pre-nationalisation colours and number — LNER 3442 — to continue its career as a preserved engine. *Neg.No.RAIL 3*

The Settle & Carlisle Line

SO MUCH has been written about this line there is little more to say here than to confirm that it opened in 1876 and the summit at Ais Gill tops out at 1,169ft above sea level. It is undoubtedly one of the most scenic lines in Britain — not in the sense of 'pretty' lines south of Bristol to the Wash, but more in the shape of great, dramatic, wild sweeps of northern moors with plunging cliffs, magnificent stone outcrops and valley — or Dale — bottoms with chequerboards of stone walls, tiny hamlets and age-old churches. The names along its route reflected the landscapes: Black Moor, Three Peaks, Simon Fell, Ais Gill, The Long Drag, Garsdale and Wild Boar Fell. Into this vast landscape came the navvies in their hundreds, with their shanty towns, boozing, fighting, sickness and — most enduring — their endeavour which created a fine railway in conditions many felt were impossible to tame. Engine crews involved in working the line were from sheds out of Sheffield, Stourton, Bradford, Skipton, Holbeck, and Hellifield; one or two sheds in Lancashire and with men from Glasgow and Carlisle working mainly the northern end.

A Leeds-based fireman who oft-stoked engines on the route once told the compiler of this book: "I've shovelled hundreds of tons of coal on that line. Every time we went over the top it felt like a victory. I suppose it made us feel a little bit proud," he added, modestly.

Taking the low road — 45605 'Cyprus' of the Jubilee Class was reduced to fast goods duty on this October day in 1962. Folks around this section of the Ribble Valley between Long Preston and Settle were expressing great concern that if a proposed reservoir for the Fylde Water Board went ahead, the railway would have to be re-laid on a new line off the right-hand edge of the picture. *Neg.N/A*

Another (almost) low road scene: A Class 5 ex-LMS 2-6-0 starts to gather speed with its train of vans on the descending gradient at Low Gill in the Lune Valley. October, 1962. *Neg.N/A.*

There are not many places in Britain in 1997 where you can stand in the middle of a road and wonder when the next train is coming: but here's a lady doing it, and leaving her Austin inconsider-ately parked half-way into the 'wrong' lane, at a point where you really start to get the idea of what a challenge the railway's builders faced. Judging by the skyline on the right of the picture, you might suppose it fell off the end of the world at that point. *Neg.N/A*

This unusual shot of the Ribblehead Viaduct (also see the 'Style Spans The Years' section of this book), was exhibited by Andrew Griffiths in an exhibition of Yorkshire landscapes at the Devonshire Arms Hotel, Bolton Abbey, in 1985. The curiously weathered stone formations in the foreground are a feature of the area near the Settle & Carlisle's longest viaduct. *Neg.N/A*

In the early 1960s, Ribblehead Viaduct underwent a massive face-lift which took three years just to complete — just 75 years after it was built. Spanning the quarter-mile wide valley between Ribblehead Station and the flanks of Whernside, it as recognised as one of the great pieces of British railway architecture. Thousands of feet of scaffolding had to be erected to allow workmen to get at the undersides of the arches and it was estimated they used 30,000 bricks to renew a complete arch. It was a tough job, especially when strong winds blew up the valley. Numerous strengthening devices had been applied to the structure, but evidence of water seepage and a need for extensive pointing was plentiful. *Neg.N/A.*

Isolated Ribblehead Station had only one platform — for southbound trains — when this picture was taken in 1992. But it was hoped to fund an additional platform by the following year with help from the public. *Neg.N/A*

The Settle & Carlisle has five viaducts, 47 cuttings, four tunnels, 67 road bridges and 100 culverts. Here's another of the viaducts at Dent Head on the climb up the winding track to Dent Station. It was a tricky task preparing foundations for all the viaducts, due to geological conditions. The builders had to tackle limestone, some slate and grit and other parts were of carbon or boulder clay. It took six and a half years to complete with a heavy cost in materials and men. It was cut, hewn and blasted through flood, bog, snow, ice, rock and sand. Donkeys provided most of the haulage. At one time more than a thousand workers were camped out on the bleak moor land, braving freakish, unpredictable weather. April, 1956. *Neg.N/A*

The scenery might look somewhat more lush at this point, but across the lines you do not have to look far to see rocky outcrops which scarred much of the route of the Settle & Carlisle. April 1991. *Neg.N/A*

Even some of the bridges had a steep slope, as the one in the middle distance, but that was no excuse for the man on the line in the left foreground deciding to take his dog for a walk over a more level structure! May, 1988. *Neg.N/A*

The Settle & Carlisle was not the only British railway to take trains into the high country. The Stainmore Summit, on the Barnard Castle to Penrith Line, was 1,370ft above sea level — 201ft higher than Ais Gill on the Settle & Carlisle. It was opened in January, 1862 and by a sad coincidence, for thousands regretted the decision, it was closed exactly a century later in January 1962. It often required two locomotives to haul trains up its steep gradients and, by another coincidence, that was also the case at Sherman Hill, Wyoming, where the Union Pacific Railroad was faced with either taking long freight trains up the hill in two sections, or needed two heavy locomotives to do it at one go. It was not until the UP introduced its mammoth 'Big Boy' engines (see 'Transatlantic Steam' elsewhere in this publication) that the company had an engine capable of doing the job on its own. Another coincidence — the compiler of this book was struck by the similarity of the terrain in this picture to that traversed by the Union Pacific in Wyoming. January 20, 1962. *Neg.N/A*

Both Sherman Hill and Stainmore Summit were marked (and still is in the case of the former) by special signs giving the elevation at that point. At Stainmore, as seen here, there was a large one on each side of the twin tracks. The Stainmore line played an important part in the transfer of coal from the mines of the north-east to Workington in the north-west. But even if trains had to be double-headed, the engines used never reached the proportions of the Union Pacific locos Weight restrictions on a viaduct on the Stainmore line prevented such developments. So the LNER's J25 0-6-0 locos were about as big as they came on double-headers. (Sherman Hill tops out at 8,013ft above sea level.) *Neg.N/A*

Transatlantic Steam

SEEING that the publisher had chosen to mention on the dustjacket the compiler's particular interest in North American railroads, the latter felt he might well 'squeeze' — although that is hardly the right word for transatlantic engines — some of his own choice into this narrative.

Hopefully, purists of British styling to the nth degree will not be offended by this mobile exhibition of the plumber's art, nor consider it 'a bit of Yankee bluster' that American purists of Union Pacific power could claim that a 'Big Boy' was so big it could run in two different states at the same time! So, as they say in San Francisco, 'Enjoy.'

Did you ever notice how, in any old-time picture, somebody's dog always managed to get itself into a prime position? But the one on this old ten-wheeler engine obviously didn't understand when the photographer called:"Everybody look this way and say 'cheese'." Maybe it had spotted a rattlesnake in the undergrowth. The Kansas City Pittsburgh & Gulf 4-6-0 had taken on a real shine for the occasion, especially its headlamp and bell. The location was Millers Bluff, Missouri, in 1893. *Collection of Harold K. Vollrath, Kansas City.*

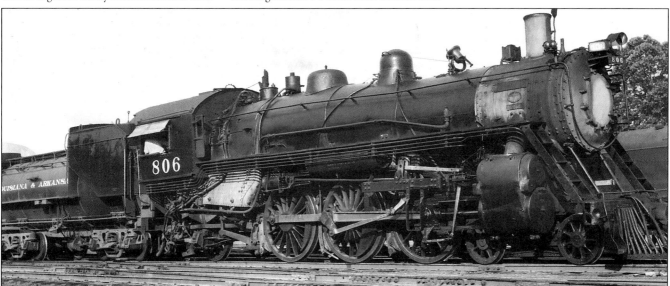

Louisiana & Arkansas 4-6-2 No.806 looked out of proportion with its Vanderbilt tender when it came into Shreveport, Louisiana, one day in May, 1949. The bell atop the Pacific's boiler was ringing well, but the massive chime whistle (looking like a hand held up for help just ahead of the cab) was silent. There were a few bumps and bruises on the ex-Kansas City Southern engine, which was built at Schenectady in 1912. The builder's plate is just about readable, above the cylinders, but the larger plate above it contained so much type you would need to be on the running board to read it. Perhaps it was one of those bank and trust company plates which said the loco would be re-possessed if the instalments on it were not paid on time! *Collection of Harold K. Vollrath, Kansas City.*

Also in Shreveport on that May day in 1949 was this pert-looking 4-6-0 No.396 of the Louisiana & Arkansas with an even bigger whistle than its rel-ative. Considering the hammering which steam locomotives in the UK and US had taken in the heavy load years during and after World War Two, this engine was in remarkably good condition. It was built by the Baldwin Locomotive Works in 1915. *Collection of Harold K. Vollrath, Kansas City.*

Environmentalists might shudder, but long before trucks and automobiles got around to polluting the highways, the railroads were doing their share, although no one seemed to bother much in those days, other than people like Aunt Eleanor from the Deep South who might have got a smut from a lo-comotive's stack on her pretty white dress as they were about to leave Chattanooga. Ironically, the great pall being blasted aloft by these two vintage locos came from burning oil; and the train they were hauling was almost completely made up of tank cars as they moved aviation gasoline and lu-bricating oil to Barksdale Air Force Base, near Shreveport, in 1942. *Picture: A.E. Brown.*

When this massive piece of railroad equipment was running full out, it looked as if everything below the running board was moving in different directions. Looking-up from below that line was rather like scanning the side of an aircraft carrier, with a mass of equipment - air tanks, trunking for the cylinders on the aft engine (yes, there are actually two sets of driving wheels, or 'engines' under the single boiler on this articulated monster) funnel, boiler-mounted sand-boxes and distributor pipes, marker lights and a rolled-up sunshade. The steps leading up to the cab were almost long enough to clean the back bedroom windows on the average Leeds back-to-back. Kansas City Southern's No.766, built by Brooks in 1929, was at Shreveport in August, 1949, with a mixed freight in tow and the brakeman, whose name was Roy Jones (you can bet his nickname was 'Casey') was riding easy on the Vanderbilt tender. The engineer, who possibly had British connections, was John Bull Harris. *Collection of Harold K. Vollrath, Kansas City.*

American and Canadian steam locomotives might have looked somewhat untidy, or rough and ready — call it what you will — in the eyes of the many British enthusiasts who liked a boiler to have a smooth cladding and to 'look like a boiler, not an organ loft' as an (English) Southern Railway fan told the compiler. But faced by the sort of weather extremes that prevail in North America, particularly in the winter, the ability to 'get at' and easily maintain as many parts of the engine as possible was a ruling factor in their design. Ladders, steps and plentiful handholds made it easier to reach air pumps, feed water heaters, lamps, bells, generators and other parts one might not have been able to reach so easily on sheathed and sophisticated British engines. The 'Sentry box' on No.510's tender was, by the way, the 'crummy' which gave the conductor or brakeman some weather protection when he wasn't out along the top of box cars turning brake wheels to apply extra braking power when required. 'Tell Tales' — strips of heavy material which hung over passing trains from a horizontal bar mounted on a trackside post — warned brakemen when to drop flat — or climb down a box car's ladder — because they were about to enter a tunnel! *Neg.N/A*

Whatever the purists might have felt, there was little doubt about it that even before the end World War Two, British, German and French locomotive designers were also thinking more about practical matters like ease of maintenance and crew comfort, and possibly less about looks. Like it or not — and she could hardly be called a 'Bonny Baby' — British Railways' Class 4F 2-6-0 (pictured here) displayed distinctive North American features: near-all-weather cab, ease of access under the high-level running plates, small diameter wheels for ease of take-off with heavy trains, and her tender's water tank shaped to allow better viability when running in reverse. *Neg.N/A*

Considering that American diesels generally enjoy a larger loading gauge than the British variety, consider how one of the latter would shape up to this huge steam job: Kansas City Southern's 2-10-4 'Texas' type No.905 with a tender the size of a double-deck bus. Built by Lima in 1937, the engine could handle long freight trains weighing several thousand tons. But the General Motors Electro-Motive Company's then standard diesel alongside it — built two years after the steam engine — was the type which was to mark the beginning of the end for North American steam power, and much of the rest of the world's steam. Significantly, the Kansas City Southern's EMD, with the lightweight 'Southern Belle' passenger cars, was overtaking the steam-powered freight. Eastwood, Missouri, September, 1948. *Collection of Harold K. Vollrath, Kansas City.*

The difference between British and American steam engines can be appreciated by this picture of the 'American Freedom Train' breasting the the tape at Alexandria, Virginia, at the start of its 21- month coast-to-coast tour of the USA during the nation's Bicentennial Year in 1976. It is still surprising to some to learn that the majority of American and Canadian trains, despite the gener- ous height and width allowed by their loading gauge, actually operate on standard gauge tracks of exactly the same width as those in Britain
Neg.N/A

Big Boy — The World's Largest Steam Locomotive

Although not a favourite of the compiler, the word 'awesome' comes readily to mind on first sighting such a monster as the Union Pacific's 'Big Boy' — reputedly the world's largest steam locomotive.

Built by the UP to haul long and heavy freight trains over 8,013ft ASL Sherman Hill, Wyoming — a task which, previously had required trains to be taken over in sections using several locomotives — this giant machine weighed 535 tons — some 200 tons more than a Boeing 747 Jumbo jet.

The engine had a 4-8-8-4 wheel arrangement; was 132ft long; 10ft 10ins wide (the overhang outside each rail was nearly 3ft); and 16ft 2ins high from rail head to the top of the double chimneys. Twenty-five of the type were built and they are said to have got their name when a construction worker chalked 'Big Boy' on the back of one of the tenders when they were in the erecting shops

The 14-wheel tender made up 86 tons of the total weight. It carried over 20,000 gallons of water, plus 28 tons of coal which was fed through an automatic stoker to the garage-size firebox. With a heavy load, a Big Boy could use up all this fuel and water on the 57-mile haul over Sherman Hill.

The enormous power of this machine can be judged by these comparisons: the tractive effort of an LMS 'Black Five' was 25,455lbs; that of an orig-inal LNER A4 'Pacific' was 35,455lbs; 'Big Boy' weighed-in with 135,375lbs of tractive effort but, even the slightly smaller Y6b 2-8-8-2 articulated engine of the Norfolk & Western generated an amazing 152,206lbs of tractive effort!

Also an articulated type, 'Big Boy' had two separate sets of pistons and driving wheels under one huge boiler. Its length was such that the Union Pacific had to restrict its use to areas where 'roundhouse' or engine shed turntables were large enough to take it and, before it went into full-time running, the radius of many sets of switches (points) had to be modified to allow the long engine to traverse them without interfering with traffic on adjoining lines.

Surprisingly, however, if clearances were sufficient, it could round fairly tight curves, as the separate sets of driving wheels followed the curve of the track whilst the long boiler appeared to swing out to one side of the line; in fact it was the driving sets moving out from under the boiler!

Such a sight was unnerving, to say the least, to the first time viewer and the compiler can confirm that even the initial climb to the vast footplate area of a Big Boy preserved at St Louis, Missouri, was a daunting task.

But he would agree with a friend — an airline vice-president who helped to pay his own way through college by standing in as a fireman on some of these huge American engines — the finest memory of Big Boy is the sheer power and sound of this mechanical dinosaur (in the lie and size sense) thundering across the plains at over 70 miles an hour, with a train a mile-and-a-half in length and its famous deep chime whistle imprinting its colossal moan over the wide open spaces.

Big Boys first went into service in 1941 but by the late 1950s even these steam giants, which had successfully contributed an enormous amount of effort to the UP's operations, were retired and their unique sound is now confined to video tapes and LPs. *Neg.N/A*

Welcome Guest Engines

If pubs famed for a regular brew can have 'guest beers' these days, we feel that a book on classic steam is perfectly entitled to include some 'guest engines' which have some relevance, even if some of them are not exactly steam. In fact, to be as fair as possible, we have included one which was a mixture of steam and diesel. Here it is:

Looking a bit like something from the Romney, Hythe & Dymchurch Railway mounted on (almost) a standard gauge frame; or perhaps a collision between a Swiss engine travelling east and an Austrian engine travelling west, this had to be one of the weirdest things on rails.

According to the original caption, this contraption is a 'steam and diesel' engine and was

built by Kitson of Leeds. It ventured on to LNER metals for trials in 1933, but they were not successful.

Of course, engineers used to say that if something looked right, it usually worked. By the same token, if it looked like ... well, various descriptions could apply to this job.

By a coincidence, when we used this picture in the Spring 1966 Edition of *Portraits of Steam*, there appeared in that same edition a letter from Mr Graham Kennewell, of Sheriff Hutton, York, asking if any reader had heard of the 'Scott Still Engine'.

He went on to say that when he was an apprentice in the 1920s, his tutor at Hull Technical College said that an example of this unique engine had been installed in a cargo boat sailing the Mediterranean.

"I am now approaching 90," he wrote, "but, so far as I know, the boat was never heard of again.

"Between the wars," he went on, "Kitson of Leeds designed a 'Still' engine which was installed in a locomotive designed for use in desert conditions, where water was in short supply.

"It had trials in Leeds, then went to York for a month, and was placed in charge of driver Percy Rosewarne. 'Still' engines had four pistons at each end and were so designed that their back ends, including the tail rod, acted as steam engines and the fronts were designed as combustion engines.

"The idea was that they started on steam and, once running, the steam was cut and oil injected: as in an internal combustion engine.

"The exhaust, instead of escaping through the chimney at the front, passed via a steam tube through the boiler to the rear end, thus maintaining the heat. The bunker held 1,000 gallons or more of water.

"The loco went on a month's trials, pulling trains between York and Doncaster [it must have confused some of the people coming out of the pubs in Selby — compiler] but although some interest was shown, the engine did not sell. The last I heard of it was that it was in Kitson's museum."

And that was pretty well that: No *Portraits of Steam* reader managed to put a finger on what actually happened to the 'Still' engine but, as the picture shows, our first guest really did exist! *Neg.No.RAIL 7*

Ask one of today's young rail fans about early British diesels and in his mind's eye he is hardly likely to picture something like this. But the first locos using this method of propulsion were shunters, such as the basic 1930s design which formed the forerunner of shunters later seen all over British railways. Other types tried included unique No.11001 which came to Yorkshire to work for three months, on loan from the Southern Region. Here it is working at Stourton, Leeds, on July 31, 1952. Despite much testing, it remained the sole example of its design; but the Class 08 type introduced the following year was built in the hundreds. *Neg.No.3/C649 (2/C649, taken from cab end is also available)*

Now, here's something that really made an impact: in August, 1956, the world's then most powerful diesel locomotive, the prototype English Electric 'Deltic', began a series of tests between Skipton and Carlisle, over a gruelling route which had often been the scene of steam trials in the past. Big and impressive, the 'Deltic' had looks reminiscent of its American counterpart — No.103 of the General Motors Electro-Motive Company, which became famous as 'the engine that did it' because its performance was such that it led the rush by American railroads to scrap their steam and go over to more efficient, less costly to run and maintain diesels. The 'Deltic' packed 3,300hp under its car body. The name, incidentally, came from the Greek letter Delta shape of its Napier marine engines. It was the forerunner of 22 Class 55 locomotives which took over London King's Cross expresses from 'Pacifics' in the early 1960s and they ran up some remarkable records. *Neg.No.J747/1. Other 'Deltic pictures are available on Neg.Nos. J950/2, D151/1, D151/2 and D151 /6. (see next picture)*

Wakefield was not exactly 'en fête' to mark the passing of the 'Deltic' prototype being tested on a wet and miserable day. Perhaps the fans were mourning the passing of steam. British Railways, on the other hand, had plenty about which to cheer: the new diesel ably demonstrated its capability of maintaining 100mph with ordinary expresses, as well as its climbing abilities with extraordinary loads on hilly routes. *Neg.No.J950/2*

The two-pronged attack on steam power in York-shire also saw it displaced by electric traction as well as diesels. The Manchester-Sheffield/Wath electrification scheme — planned by the LNER before World War Two — was finally switched on in the early 1950s, Two of its 'MSW' electrics are seen here 'on shed'. *Neg.No.8/762R*

Electric locomotives hauled passenger services over the Woodhead Tunnel route through the Pen-nines between Manchester and Sheffield until the rationalisation of the 1960s, when the line became freight only. Work on the prototype locomotive for the route was started just before World War Two and resumed following the end of hostilities. On completion, the prototype loco was lent to the Netherlands Railways to help with their shortage and to give it a thorough testing. In 1951 it was re-turned and entered British Railways' service, re-numbered 26000. It was also given nameplates carrying its Dutch nickname 'Tommy'. Under-neath the plate was a small plaque stating: 'So named by the drivers of the Netherlands State Railways, to whom this locomotive was loaned.' Pictured is another engine of the class, No.26026 with a passenger train in 1952. *Neg.No.1/762R*

Tunnel To The Dales

ON THE sort of trains that run today between Harrogate and Leeds, in a world of walkmans, mobile phones, laptop computers, thoughts of pressures of shopping (a place to sit down for even five minutes is not the first thing that comes to mind apparently when architects are planning stores these days), there will be few passengers interested in the romance of the line, or 'the poor sods' as they were often called, who had the job of building it.

Yet had it not been for the navvies prepared to risk their lives boring, digging and blasting the then stinking hole of Bramhope Tunnel, road congestion between Harrogate and Leeds would be even more hideous than it is today.

As it was, more than 30 workmen died in the task of creating that two-mile 241 yards hole in the ground. It might not be the country's longest tunnel — it ranks about eighth — but the conditions facing the constructors were among the most appalling.

The water that caused most of the trouble originated (and still does) on the East Chevin above Otley with a kink in the Pennine strata forcing it eastward, when a few hundred yards would have seen it flowing the other way, toward Guiseley, of Harry Ramsden's Fish & Chip shop fame.

Those 30 workmen and scores more came from all over Britain; many from as far away as Ireland. A memorial to those who lost their lives stands on the north side of Otley churchyard. They worked in dreadful conditions, ever wary of roof falls from the treacherous strata, to drive the line under Bramhope, where an air shaft that used to vent smoke and fumes still stands alongside the A660 road from Leeds to Skipton.

Not far away, at the junction of Moor Road and Moorland Road, are the remains of a siting tower used by surveyors planning the line of the tunnel.

Hundreds of years before them the locals, wary of the Romans, had a camp almost directly over where the line of the tunnel would run beneath those two roads.

In the early days, locomotives of the then Leeds & Thirsk Railway line (authorised in 1845 and later known as the 'Leeds Northern') were not far in advance of the world-famed 'Rocket'. Many of them tackled the tunnel with the majority of their passengers in conveyances little better than open trucks used for goods traffic.

Lack of engine power and the conditions in the tunnel led to many incidents: among them was a serious accident when a heavily-laden passenger train stalled on the greasy lines, reversed back down to Arthington so that the driver could 'take a run' at the tunnel but his train was struck from behind by another train before he could do so.

The years have softened the approaches to the tunnel, particularly at the northern (Harrogate) end, where, as can be seen in some of these pictures, the 'environmentally friendly' tunnel mouth and a mass of mature trees make for something of an idyllic appearance.

The memorial, on the north side of Otley Parish churchyard, to over 30 men who died working on the Bramhope tunnel project. *Neg.No.BIW98*

Victorian landowners were often 'sweetened' by railway companies which provided ornate structures to make their rights of permanent way more acceptable environmentally. What a pity, therefore, that after going to all that trouble to provide a proud and pleasant tunnel mouth at the the Wharfedale end of Bramhope Tunnel, someone years later saw fit to erect what looks like a Colorado mountain man's shack on the right. Meanwhile, well-named A3 No.60081 'Shotover' shoots out of the tunnel, its fireman eager for a breath of fresh air, as it speeds toward Arthington Viaduct and Harrogate beyond in February, 1958. *Neg.No.BIW 84*

Clear of the dripping hole in the ground, engine No.60071, aptly named 'Tranquil', is bathed in sunshine and the glorious Wharfedale atmosphere as it gathers speed on the downgrade into Arthington. June, 1957. *Neg.No.BIW 73*

Further down the line, a year later to the month, No.60074 — another A3, named 'Harvester' — is also well-named to match the rural background as it comes down to meet the Otley/Ilkley branch coming in from the right. *Neg.No.BIW 29*

The Otley branch is in the right foreground and Arthington Station is left in the haze of the locomotive's exhaust as B1 No.61035 'Pronghorn' hurries a Leeds-Northallerton train, with a fine mix of coaches, on its way in July, 1959. *Neg.No.BIW 76*

Another B1, No.61084, slows to take a special (amply identified by the number 589 chalked on both buffers and the smoke box door) on to the Otley/Ilkley line, whose radius or 'degree' listing is emphasised by the lengthy check rails inside the nearside running rails of the twin track branch. This was in March 1957. *Neg.No.BIW 75*

It's a frosty morning as this former LNER engine hauls a rake of quite fascinating ex-LNER bogies around the Otley-Harrogate loop of the triangular junction at Arthington. Coaches six and seven feature the centrally-located oval windows that marked the toilets of some mixed-class coaches. The number 599 chalked on the smoke box door suggests the train might have been a special; more than likely bound for a race meeting. *Neg.N/A*

This picture completes the set on Arthington's triangular junction. The main station buildings were inside the triangle of lines and 2-6-2 Class 3P tank loco No.40140 (whose back end has the look of some equipment on a German armoured train of World War Two), has come from Ilkley, via Otley, and is exiting the Leeds platform to take the main Harrogate-Leeds line up to Bramhope Tunnel. The two coaches on this local were better turned-out than the engine in the March, 1958 shot, but the footplate crew had the satisfaction that at least they would have some reasonably decent air to breath whilst their loco's smoke enveloped the carriages on their way up to Horsforth. *Neg.No.BIW 49*

The Assault on Bramhope

THE previous section deposited readers on the doorstep of Wharfedale — not a place that leaps to mind when today's railway enthusiasts (even Yorkshire born) are asked where you could once see some unusual railway activity.

Yet all the evidence is still there to see — and some of the tracks are still in use in and around the village of Arthington. Something of a sun trap in summer and often ice-bejewelled in winter; with an assortment of distant steeples and views of the splendours at the gateway to the Dales, Arthington has seen its moments of glory, excitement and tragedy.

All three were generated by the great hole (described in the previous section) that bores into the eastern extremity of Otley Chevin to carry the Harrogate-Leeds line upward through the dripping rock to emerge near an ancient farm between the once mysterious woods of Cookridge and the wind-shorn Pennine spur that now hosts the Leeds Bradford International Airport.

Great expresses to and from points such as London, Edinburgh, Newcastle, Liverpool, Ripon, Harrogate and Leeds were regular users of the tunnel; as were local trains which got to and from it via the triangle of lines that marked Arthington.

What a joy it was on a summer's evening to take a drink at the 'Wharfedale', then watch these great trains curving round that magnificent 21-arch viaduct, safety valves blowing off when heading north-east; of the fireman working up a sweat as he shovelled to enable his engine to make the assault on that great black hole, hoping that the seemingly ever-present drips or rivulets of water would not cause 'slippage' to slow the journey towards Leeds.

Most trains on the Otley-Leeds line via Arthington were of the lighter type and the gradient through the tunnel did not give them too many problems. But on the main Harrogate-Leeds line through Arthington, expresses with 11 or 12 'bogies', or coaches, were the norm so it was not unusual to see a good deal of double-headed working, especially on Newcastle-Liverpool trains. In this view, from just above a driver's eye level of the 'Down' main line at the north-eastern apex of the Arthington triangle, a post indicates a falling gradient of one in 94 as the main line takes a set of shallow reverse curves (an 'S' bend to motorists) before reaching Arthington Viaduct.
The lane from the main Harewood Bridge-Pool and Otley road comes up on the left to Arthington Station, passing under a bridge which carried the Harrogate-Otley-Ilkley loop line (in foreground, curving off to the left). Directly ahead is a small siding opposite Arthington North signal box, with cattle-loading dock where the single van is standing. The small stone building on the left was probably where livestock could be held overnight for early morning departures.

And the train making its assault on the gradient up to Bramhope Tunnel? It was a Newcastle-Liverpool express, pictured in February, 1958, with A3 No.60085 'Manna' leading the charge. *Neg.No.BIW 68*

Storming round the left-hand curve to line-up for its tunnel dash in April, 1957, A3 No.60060 'The Tetrarch' has a train of BR standard maroon coaches in tow, Signs of cut-backs to come lie in the rail-less sleepers with piles of 'chairs' and fishplates in the foreground, ready for removal. *Neg.No.BIW 41*

Exhaust barking, unburnt coal dust flying, the distant Almscliffe Crag almost lost to sight, 'fireman busy on the poop deck,' as one old Leeds driver used to say. The evening sun lowers over the dale as A3 No.60076 gallops into the straight and, á la Goodwood, heads up the hill for a thundering passage through Bramhope Tunnel. And the engine's name? Would you believe 'Galopin'. The year — 1958. *Neg.No.BIW 71*

A summer evening, in June, 1958, as a special train with a fine assortment of coaches is powered by A1 No.60141 'Abbotsford', no doubt its off-beat exhaust noted by the locals in the tap room at the 'Wharfedale' below Arthington's large embankment. Note the old-style swivel shunting signal in the foreground. *Neg.No.BIW 47*

Not a 'Tally Ho!' to be heard, but plenty of mechanical motion as D49 'Hunt' Class 'The Quorn' double-heads an unidentified A3 as train engine, with a heavy consist of coaches in May, 1950. *Neg.No.BIW 11*

Hunters of railwayana would kill today for some of this stuff: a real water column, a genuine shed, a cast-iron notice to passengers; and a 'kink' in the line on the left. The fireman of B1 No.61321 has done his stuff, judging by the chimney, and has time to eye the photographer from the footplate as the old gal shakes, rattles and rolls a Harrogate to King's Cross train through Arthington in July, 1958, the gradient already making itself felt.
Neg.No.BIW 70

These five sets of points represented the nearest Arthington Station got to being 'the Waterloo of Wharfedale' as an unidentified V2 2-6-2 steamed hard past the station's water tank, hauling a Newcastle-Liverpool express. Curving in from the right is the line from/to Otley and Ilkley. It was July, 1959, and there was a whiff of diesel in the air as the new-fangled 'mechanical boxes' started to appear on some of the branch lines around Leeds.
Neg.No.BIW 77

The view from the other side of the junction, with the 25mph Otley/Ilkley line running off to the left and Arthington's station buildings in the middle distance. Well-equipped to tackle gradient and tunnel, the express has B16 No.61452 double-heading an unidentified A3 'Pacific' as train engine. *Neg.No.BIW 23*

A clear July morning in 1959 as British Railways Standard 4-6-0 No.73168 is caught by the camera with a rake of Pullman rolling stock. *Neg.No.BIW 79*

Finally, memories are made of this — a last look at trains in glorious Wharfedale. With Almscliffe Crag topping the skyline, the gloom of Bramhope Tunnel is still some two miles ahead as A3 No.60081 'Shotover' takes 'The Queen of Scots' Pullman through Weeton and Huby on the Harrogate-Leeds line on May 16, 1952. A fitting finale to a parade of splendid trains through a piece of splendid countryside. *Neg.No.10/C635*